A BEAVER IS
EATING MY CANOE

True Tales to make you Laugh, Chortle, Snicker and Feel Inspired

Edited by Matt Jackson

Summit Studios

Library and Archives Canada Cataloguing in Publication

A beaver is eating my canoe : true tales to make you laugh, chortle, snicker and feel inspired / edited by Matt Jackson.

ISBN 978-0-9734671-6-1

1. Outdoor life--Canada--Humor. I. Jackson, Matt
PN6178.C3B43 2008   796.5'0971   C2008-903313-2

Designed by Kirk Seton, Signet Design Inc.
Cover Photo by Robert McCaw
Printed and bound in Canada

SUMMIT STUDIOS
#105, 2572 Birch St.
Vancouver, British Columbia
V6H 2T4 Canada

This book is dedicated to all travellers who

venture forth bravely and come home

with stories to share

Table of Contents

Introduction

By Matt Jackson

The beaver is Canada's national animal. It is also a web-footed, bucktoothed, semi-aquatic rodent that on land is prone to waddling around in an ungainly fashion between water's edge and forest. It is shy and retiring. It has long, sprouting whiskers and a wide, flat tail. True, the beaver is the largest member of the rodent family—an adult can weigh upwards of sixty pounds—but it is still considered small compared to other mammals. Many Canadians believe that it has a decided lack of sex appeal.

Why then has our country chosen the beaver as its national animal? Why not claim the majestic polar bear, the cunning wolf, or the roving caribou as our symbol? Would these animals not better exemplify the pride, the strength, the intelligence, and the spirit of the Canadian people?

Some will point out that the beaver is industrious, and that may be all well and good. But let me ask you this: Would *you* want to be a waddling, web-footed, bucktoothed midget, even if your neighbors regularly admitted, "Oh, but he's so studious!"

There is, however, a lesser-known side to this timid animal. Beavers can be as aggressive and territorial as any critter, and I've heard of more than one unsuspecting canoeist who has coloured their underwear when a brown-furred, miniature Jaws has launched itself from the water beside their boat, two incisors arcing through the air like lethal weapons. I've also read about a beaver from Norway that successfully took out a tour bus by chewing down a tree next to a major highway. The bus driver saw the tree falling across the road and swerved to avoid hitting it, but couldn't prevent it from broadsiding the bus, shattering a window and hospitalizing one passenger.

There is also the beaver American Ken Penland encountered during a quiet paddle down the C&O canal on the Maryland side of the Potomac River. Penland was happily paddling his prized wood-canvas canoe—a boat he had just spent more than three hundred hours refurbishing—when he encountered what can only be described as a demon beaver. You'll find the tale of Penland's epic struggle in "A Taste for the Classics."

As with our previous short story collections (*Mugged by a Moose* and *I Sold My Gold Tooth for Gas Money*), we have assembled in this edition several more dollops of delightful, dramatic, and occasionally bizarre anecdotes. They span a wide spectrum. Along with Penland's tale of woe in the "travel fiascoes" category, Leslie Bamford takes us on another trip with her (overly) adventurous husband in "Siren Eyes," inviting us along to watch as things go terribly wrong. Again! Not that Leslie is one shade bitter about it. These misadventures, after all, give her something to write about.

Another of my favourites in this "mobile mishaps" vein— which features BC truck driver Brian Andersen delivering farm goods across the U.S. border—is only loosely related to travel.

Nevertheless, his story "Holy Crap" was so unusual that we simply had to include it.

You'll also find high adventure between these pages. Brent Curry writes about a thousand-plus kilometre winter bicycle trip above the Arctic Circle. Ron Johnson survives a long night on a tropical island that turns out to be anything but his fantasy. And Jason Hoerle pens a tale about his "daring" escape (as a tourist) from Bolivia's dangerous San Pedro prison.

Along with the laughs and thrill rides, we've also included a few stories more likely to inspire a moment of reflection or a sense of wonder. One of the most memorable for me is "Freeze Frame" by Jennifer Ball, a simple story about a day trip she took with her mom as a teenager, and how a single event from that day has crystallized into memories that have stood the test of time. Ball's theme is one that is often overlooked in travel literature: sometimes it's not the places we visit that are most memorable, but rather the people we travel with.

An equally poignant story is "After the Flood" by Julie Siebt. It's the unbelievable account of Julie and her husband Ken travelling around the world in 2004 with their two daughters, aged nine and eleven—only to land in Railay Bay, Thailand for Christmas. The next day, on December 26th, the deadliest tsunami in recorded history swept in from the Indian Ocean, ravaging the quiet community (and the country) they had been visiting. It's an event that has since changed their lives in ways they never thought possible.

Travel does that: it changes us. Could this be why we brave the many discomforts of the road and the Great Outdoors? Perhaps it's because life-altering experiences seem easier to find—and personal transformation easier to achieve—when we're not in familiar surroundings, bound by the rules and routines of home. We want to be changed. We *yearn* to be changed. So we travel, hoping to catch a glimpse of something bigger and brighter inside ourselves. And our landscape of choice, though it may contribute to this change, is often secondary.

This, I believe, is why a destination that deeply moves one person, bringing them back year after year, may fail completely to inspire the next traveller. For the changed person, the place is forever associated with the transformation that occurred within them; the place is now a *part* of that person.

Of course, if you happen to be touring the countryside of northern Norway, it's always possible the bus you're riding in could be transformed into a heap of scrap. I guess the brochures forgot to mention the demon beavers. They change everything.

Cougar Fanny

Under siege at Pretty Girl Lake.

By Wayne Van Sickle

It was spring of my third year at the University of Waterloo. I was plugging away at a degree in Mathematics, and exams were fast approaching. I probably should have been talking with Professor Furino about Combinatorics and Optimization, or seeking enlightenment during Professor Vanstone's office hours. But my mind was concerned with a problem far more personally relevant: what to do the week after school let out.

A friend and classmate named Edson called with the beginnings of a solution. He had two weeks free after his exams and suggested we fly to Vancouver Island to go hiking in Strathcona Provincial Park. I agreed immediately, and decided that since I had three weeks between the end of school and the start of my summer job, I would stay out there for the extra week. What would I do?

The possibilities for adventure were endless, and all were far more engaging than studying for final exams. I had recently read a magazine article about sea kayaking the Broken Group Islands in Pacific Rim National Park: the story had images of the West Coast forests, giant moon snails, sea cucumbers, starfish and First Nations artifacts. I was hooked. I decided that a solo kayaking trip on the

Pacific Ocean was exactly the right way to spend my extra week.

And so, while I should have been reviewing my math notes, I instead got on the phone to order nautical charts for the park and reserve a kayak at a West Coast outfitter.

Exams came and went, and I was soon hiking in the backcountry of Strathcona Park with Edson. At camp one day, I spread out the nautical charts, chose my route, picked campsites, and made a menu. I pictured myself paddling through Pacific waters in a bright yellow kayak. It was all very exciting.

Yet some details I had overlooked were beginning to nag at me. What had seemed like "small" details when considered from a distance now seemed very important less than a week away from my first solo kayaking trip on the Pacific. The biggest of these details was the fact that I had never actually been in a kayak and had no experience whatsoever with the ocean. I had paddled canoes in Ontario many times, but wasn't the ocean different? An undeniable sense of doubt grew in me as I looked closely at the marine charts and noted that there was absolutely nothing between the campsite I had selected for night four and the islands of Japan.

It was time to consider other options. It occurred to me that I could sign up for a guided trip, but I quickly dismissed that idea as too pricey for my student budget. Plus, I wasn't sure about a trip with strangers. I liked to do things on my own, or with friends. I resolved to learn about the ocean another day and return for that kayak trip then. That left me with the question of what to do for those extra seven days.

After returning from Strathcona and waving goodbye to Edson as his bus left for Victoria, I walked to a phone booth and called the kayak company, explaining my lack of experience and comfort with the whole ocean idea. They weren't too impressed by my last-minute enlightenment, but they didn't try to convince me to take their boat out either. I suppose they figured it could be bad for business if someone they rented a kayak to disappeared and washed up seven months later on the shores of Iwo Jima.

Much to my surprise, however, they didn't offer me a refund on my deposit. This left me standing in a phone booth on Vancouver Island with a pile of camping equipment, eight days to kill before my return flight home, exactly $237.56, and no superhero costume to change into. For lack of better ideas, I began to flip through the Yellow Pages. The phone book was pretty slim and it wasn't long belong I got to "Airlines." A black and yellow ad jumped out at me—an airline from Gold River was advertising affordable charter service to anywhere on Vancouver Island.

So I did exactly what the circumstances begged me to do: I phoned the airline and told them I was on the island with no plans because "the goddamn kayak company I reserved with totally messed up my reservation and didn't have a boat for me." I asked them if there were any remote and wild places, far away from civilization, where they might possibly drop me by float plane, leave me on my own, and pick me up a week later. Taking a quick second breath, I added that I could pay them not more than $237.31 ($237.56 minus the twenty-five cents invested in the phone call).

I expected to hear laughter followed by a dial tone. Instead, the man who had answered said, "I think we may have something for you." He went on to tell me about Pretty Girl Lake, which sounded exactly like what I was looking for: a remote wilderness lake that was just about as far into the middle of nowhere as one could get on Vancouver Island. The pilots flew out to it themselves whenever they wanted a break.

"There are no pretty girls at Pretty Girl Lake," said the man, "but there's a fire pit, an old rowboat, and a table built into the side of a tree." My spirits lifted. This was exactly the wind I needed beneath my wings. I may not have known anything about ocean currents, tides, and nautical charts, but I knew how to operate a rowboat, and I was extremely proficient with a table. Pretty Girl Lake sounded perfect!

There was one catch. It takes a lot of fuel for a float plane to take off, fly out to the middle of nowhere, land on a lake, take off again, return to the dock, and then do the whole thing again a week later. There would be no profit to be made in offering this service for $237.31.

But the creativity of private enterprise knows no limits, and the man informed me that they could provide me with this service for said price as long as my schedule was flexible. They couldn't make a special trip out to the lake to drop me off, but if I was willing to wait, they would get me into a float plane as soon as they received a request for a charter that would take them anywhere in the vicinity of Pretty Girl Lake. In this way, they wouldn't have to burn any extra fuel or airtime; they could simply drop me off as they flew by the lake on other business.

The flexibility I was required to show came into play because the charter request could come five minutes after my arrival at the docks, or it could take two days before someone wanted to go that way. The game for being picked up after my stay at the lake would be played in roughly the same manner: they would wait six days and then swoop down unannounced onto the lake the first time they were overhead on a job for someone paying full price. The pick-up flight could come as early as the afternoon of day six or as late as day eight.

I arrived in the tiny village of Gold River the next morning with enough time to grab a quick breakfast at the local cafe before heading down to the docks. I picked up a local newspaper and read it as I ate. One headline commanded more attention than the others: "Boy Loses Scalp to Cougar."

There are no grizzly bears on Vancouver Island, but there are plenty of cougars. Many people will tell you that cougars are more dangerous than the great brown bear because they have been known to stalk humans as prey. That's exactly what had happened in Gold River the day before my arrival. A cougar had jumped over a hedge onto the sidewalk and pounced on a young boy who was walking to school. If not for the immediate intervention of several adults, who beat the cougar off, the boy wouldn't have escaped with his life.

As I strolled down to the docks after breakfast, I made sure to walk in the middle of the road, far from any hedges.

I introduced myself to the pilots, then set up my Crazy Creek foldable chair on the adjacent beach and started reading while awaiting the call. Late in the afternoon, a charter request came in; I was summoned and, moments later, was in the air flying off into the remote interior of Vancouver Island.

From the window of the plane, I saw countless lakes and huge tracts of forest. I spotted a black bear rambling through the woods, and the conversation turned to the subject of island wildlife. When I mentioned the boy who had been attacked by the cougar, the pilot told me they were having a "bad cougar year" in town. Apparently, one had menaced him from underneath the stairs of his porch; he had pulled out his gun and shot it.

The pilot nudged me as Pretty Girl Lake came into sight. The immediate surroundings were hilly and forested in all directions, with no roads or signs of civilization anywhere. The float plane landed and taxied to the shoreline, and I stepped out of the cabin with my gear. After the pilot took off, I could hear the plane's engine for only a few moments before it disappeared from view.

And then I was alone.

There was no moon that first night, and the stargazing far surpassed any other night I could remember. I could practically reach out and touch the Milky Way. I built a fire and settled in for an evening of contemplation, but it's not easy to contemplate when your thoughts are drowned out by frogs. It was spring, and the croaking of the amphibian community was loud and impressive.

I am no frogologist, but I have noticed that frogs on each of the four continents I have visited act remarkably similar at night.

They carry on with their loud croaking just long enough for me to tune it out, and then they come to a complete and sudden stop—not just one or two frogs, but every single one of them. The dead silence they leave behind can feel a bit unsettling, especially when you're by yourself; have they detected the approach of a threat? I'm not the only creature that experiences distress in this situation—I've seen full-grown rhinos in Africa panic when the frogs stop croaking. And sometimes, when I have camped beside water, I will wake up in the middle of the night to this silence, and be unable to fall back to sleep.

The frogs made it through that first night, and so did I.

Over the course of the next few days, I swam frequently and took numerous hikes around the lake and up and down its associated streams. I enjoyed quiet time looking at plants, sketching, reading, or lying on my stomach to get an up-close view of the world as ants see it.

On day two I saw a grouse beating its wings, and managed to walk right up to it before it saw me.

Sometime in the afternoon of the third day, I realized that I had not uttered a noise of any kind for two days. There is something very worthwhile about being silent for long periods of time in nature. It deepens one's connection to the land.

After four days alone, not having seen another person or spoken a single word, I felt more in tune with the forest than ever before. Hiking that day, I could hear the soft and regular *thump, thump, thump* of my heartbeat.

I began and ended each day with a skinny-dip in the lake. On the sixth day, as I sauntered up to the shore after my morning swim, I found myself questioning the point of putting my clothes back on. After all, I was in the middle of nowhere entirely by myself. I had seen the total remoteness of my surroundings from the plane trip in, and there was absolutely no risk of anybody seeing me. Even if the plane came back, I would have plenty of warning. I would be able to hear it from miles away.

I couldn't have been more wrong.

Going about life without clothes on takes a bit of getting used to. For example, while making tea for myself, I admit to feeling a bit unsettled about having my dangling bits so close to the open flame of my cookstove. But for the most part it was wonderful, and soon I was back in my Crazy Creek chair, rocking gently back and forth, happily lost in my book.

Then a flicker of movement caught my eye. I lifted my head to see a fuzzy housecat on the shore about ten metres away from me. This failed to hold my attention, because I was totally engrossed in the story I was reading. After all, seeing a housecat is an everyday occurrence—nothing to write home about. I put my head back down and kept reading. But I couldn't get back into the book, and it wasn't for being naked; something else just didn't seem quite right.

I leaned back in my chair to consider things, and as I did, I happened to look over and see the cat again. It had advanced upon me to a point roughly five metres away. It was crouched low, wiggling its behind the way cats do when they are about to pounce on something. Apparently the cute little thing thought it was going to catch me. I wasn't too worried because, after all, I'm much bigger than a mouse. I smiled at the cat in a patronizing type of way.

That's when I snapped out of my daydream. My eyes grew as big as saucers, the rocking in my chair ceased, and I froze. I remembered that I was in the middle of nowhere. There were no houses within miles, and therefore no housecats. This kitten, quite clearly, was a cougar kitten! The young cougar was probably learning how to stalk and pounce on prey. Either it had run off from its mother, or she was behind me this very moment watching her young one, ready to come in herself and demonstrate the proper mauling and gutting technique. My scalp tingled.

In a moment like this, a man learns where he fits in on the "fight or flight" continuum. Adrenaline surged into my bloodstream and without a moment's thought I picked up my small fishing knife, stood up, wheeled around, and let out the most horrific blood-curdling scream of aggression.

The good news was that there was nothing behind me. The bad news was that wherever the mother cougar happened to be, she now knew where I was, and that she was missing her kitten. She would, without a doubt, be emerging from the trees momentarily.

I took up a wide-legged stance and waited. As the adrenaline subsided and my body sent blood back to my brain, my intellect came back on line. I reconsidered the situation. Clearly, I was not a perfectly honed fighting machine; I was a naked man standing on a remote beach with a small fishing knife in his hand.

And so I did what hundreds of thousands of years of human evolution have prepared me to do in such a crisis. I ran down the beach, dived into the rowboat, paddled like there was no tomorrow, and didn't stop until I reached the middle of the lake. There, I took a deep breath, looked up at the fluffy clouds, and thanked the skies for letting me escape alive. I was safe.

I calmed myself down and things slowly returned to normal— as normal as things could be, that is, for a naked man sitting in a rowboat waiting for a plane.

As I drifted there in my rowboat, a number of questions floated to the forefront of my mind. The first thing I considered was what I would do if the plane didn't come that day. Should I sleep in the boat or try going back to the tent?

Equally intriguing was what might happen if the plane did in fact come that day. What were the chances the pilot would actually land on Pretty Girl Lake after looking down from his pre-landing pass to see a naked man in a rowboat? Would he be tempted to report me as missing and let the Mounties sort things out?

The third and most burning question was: "Why didn't I apply sunscreen before sitting down to read?"

The stress of the whole incident and the coming down off the adrenaline high had left me completely tired out. There was no wind on the lake and the water was calm, so I decided to have a nap and reassess things in a few hours.

When I woke up, things were much the same: calm lake, nice clouds, no cougar. It was probably safe to go back on land, but for obvious reasons, I hesitated.

And that's when I heard the droning engine of the float plane.

If the people from Guinness had been there, I would no doubt be the current world record holder for naked rowing. I was taking no chances on the pilot leaving me behind. By the time the plane approached the lake for its pre-landing circle, I was already nearing the shore. By the time he was overhead, I was on shore. And at the very moment the plane touched down on the lake, I was frantically pulling on a pair of pants.

As the pilot stepped out of the plane's cabin and onto the pontoons, I was throwing the last of my camping gear into my backpack. I walked down to the water's edge just as he was jumping to shore. If he had noticed me naked out there in the rowboat, he didn't mention it.

He taxied the plane for takeoff, and as we rose up over the hills he turned to me and asked, "See any wildlife?"

I paused before answering.

"Just a grouse and some frogs," I muttered. We flew in silence the rest of the way to Gold River.

*Despite all the distractions, Wayne Van Sickle finished his Mathematics degree. He is the author of two best-selling guidebooks to Algonquin Provincial Park in Ontario. He currently lives in Ottawa, where he teaches at a French Immersion elementary school and runs a small publishing company called Stonecutter Press. He's been back to Vancouver Island several times, but to this day has never participated in another naked rowing event. He can be reached at **stonecut@hotmail.com**.*

When Boys Become Giants

*Or how an Englishman lost his mind in the
Japanese Alps.*

By Philip Blazdell

The weather was balmy outside my Japanese hotel. The night
was still and calm, with only a light easterly wind blowing
beneath a smattering of clouds.

Dawn was a few hours away, and I was tiptoeing around the
hotel with a forty-foot Internet cable, a borrowed laptop, a six-pack
of Japanese beer, and a box of sushi. The night manager watched
curiously as I scurried back and forth.

My idea was simple: I planned to run a cable out my room
window and take the laptop I had borrowed a few hours before to
the edge of the rice field. There I could sit and listen to The Game
in peace. Tonight, of all nights, I couldn't promise to refrain from
shouting and screaming and keeping the entire hotel awake.

I had just made myself comfortable, squatting down Asian
style, when the night manager wandered over. He paused for a
second as if to assess my mood.

"You could," he told me in slow, precise Japanese, "watch
the game on TV like a civilized person." This made me so happy
I wanted to kiss him.

We returned to the hotel and pulled the TV from reception out onto the back veranda. I cracked a Kirin beer, and while the manager fiddled with the aerial, I leaned on the veranda, watched fireflies skim across the rice fields, and wished I was in Istanbul.

I am not merely mad about the Liverpool Football Club, or The Reds, as they are otherwise known. I am not *just* a fan who follows his team around the world. Rather, The Reds are the air I breathe, the blood pumping through my veins, the very beat of my heart. All my life I have followed the team. Friends come and go, lovers break my heart and leave, and I wander the globe aimlessly while my heart and soul rest at Anfield Stadium. After twenty long and frustrating years in the wilderness of mediocrity, we have finally made it to the European Cup Final, which we'll play against AC Milan. And I should be there! Tragically, I had been minutes away from booking my ticket to Istanbul when my boss thrust another plane ticket into my hand and sent me spinning off to Japan.

I shook my head wistfully, downed a swallow of beer, and sighed. I kissed my red shirt and turned my focus to the game, which was about to start.

"So who are we supporting?" asked the manager. "Red or White?"

"Red!" I cried, pointing to my shirt.

The game started. Just fifty-two seconds later Milan scored and we're down 1–0. I ground my teeth, swore in several languages, and bit my lip. This was not in the script.

"Can we support the Whites?" asked the manager. I considered going Clockwork Orange on him, but fixed him with a glacial stare instead.

The next forty-four minutes were the worst of my life. Our fragile defense crumbled and we were soon down 3–0. I tried to hide my tears from the manager.

At halftime we split the sushi box between us. I paced, fretted, ground my teeth. Anger and frustration as I have never known flooded through me. The manager watched me with a degree of reservation. Clearly he was not used to seeing a *gaijin* in such mortal pain. He wanted to reach out and offer me solace, but he didn't have the vocabulary.

"Gomen nasai?" he offered philosophically. *What can be done?*

What could be done, indeed? I opened another Kirin Ichiban beer and the second half kicked off.

Dawn was seeping over the Japanese Alps, which were covered in fresh snow, and if I hadn't already been crying, this exquisite view might have moved me to tears. Mist rolled lazily over the paddies, and bullfrogs began to croak. The first early risers were shuffling through the quaint little hotel looking for breakfast, clip-clopping around reception in their wooden shoes. Slowly, like moths drawn to a light, they gravitated toward the TV and one ranting, red-shirted Englishman.

And then Gerrard unleashed a thunderbolt and the ball struck the back of Milan's net. It was 3–1.

I exploded. I jumped up, screamed, spilled beer all over myself, kissed the manager, and almost knocked the TV set into the paddy field. My screams shattered the crystalline dawn.

As more Japanese guests were drawn toward the television, I offered a running commentary in Japanese: "Xabi to Garcia to Smicer … GOAL!" Forty-five Japanese people danced wildly with me. The score was 3–2. I punched the air, called my father on my cellphone and screamed down the phone at him. The breakfast service stopped and the hotel's focus shifted toward the television.

I was still screaming in Japanese and going wild when a Reds player was cruelly chopped down in the box.

Penalty! I couldn't watch.

I gripped the arm of a stranger and prayed. Forty-five people sucked in air. Collectively we *willed* Xabi to smack the ball into the back of the net.

He shot.

The keeper saved it.

Xabi pounced.

The ball flew into the back of the net.

The camera panned to the end of the stadium where the Reds fans were assembled; they were going berserk. I kissed the person next to me (female this time, I noted thankfully) and cried tears of joy. Across this small, sleepy town deep in the Japanese Alps, the chant of "Xabi! Xabi! Xabi Alonso!" rang loud and true. I imagined the sound throbbing over the Alps, across Asia, and floating through the Bosporus Strait to Istanbul. Complete strangers were hugging each other, spraying beers around, and patting me on my back. I felt like I had put the ball in the back of the net myself.

The manager lit another cigarette, passed me a beer, and winked at me as if to say: *I too am Red, through and through.*

The next thirty minutes shredded my nerves. Tension rippled through the crowd like a shark swimming through a calm pool. I felt alive, wired—every nerve jangled and chimed. I hadn't even been this nervous the day I stood in the delivery room and waited for my son to be born. Every touch of the ball by a Red player provoked an "Ole!" from Japan to Istanbul. We all edged closer to the game.

One of the waitresses, beautiful in her silk kimono, whispered in my ear that she thought Xabi was dreamy. I agreed with her and she giggled demurely. I noticed that her lips were the same shade of red as my shirt.

As the clock ticked down, I felt myself radiate with energy. I couldn't stand still. People gravitated toward me. It's moments like this, I realized, that new religions start. The crowd gathered on the veranda was sharing a rare moment of cosmic significance with me. Souls mingled. Dreams were shared. The dawn crackled with energy. Booze, sex, chocolate cake—nothing has ever come close to this feeling, and nothing ever will.

When the full-time whistle blew, it was cathartic. I breathed deeply.

"What happens now?" asked a salaryman who was clearly going to be late for work.

"Extra time," I informed him.

The sun finally crested the mountains. Elderly ladies, resplendent in conical hats, waddled into the rice paddies to tend to their crops. The veranda was now jammed and we all moved closer to the TV. I resumed my commentary, although I could barely speak. Ninety minutes of screaming and ranting had left me hoarse and emotionally denuded.

As the clock ticked down, the tension mounted. The dawn had a complex scent that I struggled to identify. I could smell … what? Fear? Adrenaline? Hope? All mixed with the loamy smells of a sleepy Japanese mountain town. My senses tingled and I felt acutely aware of everything happening around me.

In the dying seconds, Jerzy (our goalie) pulled off two incredible saves. For the first time since the game started I didn't feel afraid. I wore my soaked red shirt with pride and passion.

The final period of extra time was limp and lifeless; the players, like the spectators, looked spent and emotionally damaged. Penalties seemed inevitable. The final whistle blew and I cracked open my last beer. I quickly explained the rules to the Japanese while the goalkeepers prepared. Each team is awarded five kicks to start and they take them in altering sequence. If the teams are still tied after five kicks, it's down to sudden death.

I turned my focus to the game and felt Japan slide away. I was *in* Istanbul. I was *there*—heart beating, palms damp with fear. This was as close to the edge as I had ever been. I had to remind myself to breathe. I focused myself down to one single conscious thought: *We will win!*

The Whites missed the first penalty kick. So did the Reds.

The Whites missed again. The Reds smacked the back of the net with the second kick. Yes! Everyone celebrated!

The Whites missed. I realized that I was crouched with my head in my hands, my nose almost pressed to the screen.

The Reds missed. I burst into tears again.

The Whites scored. I swore and the manager patted me on the back.

The Reds scored again.

This was the moment of truth. It was the last kick for the Whites.

They missed!

I detonated like a bomb. I screamed and I ranted. Froth bubbled from my open mouth. I vaulted off the veranda, ripped off my shirt and ran screaming into the morning. I dove headfirst into the soggy rice paddy and tobogganed through the rice with wild abandon. I cried uncontrollably while kissing my shirt like it was a long-lost lover.

My screams shattered the illusion of unity and the magic passed. The Japanese on the veranda watched me shyly, rubbed their brows, and blinked as though awaking from a Cinderella dream. People began drifting off to breakfast or work.

I helped the manger shift the TV back into reception and we shook hands—older, wiser, and happier after sharing such a night.

Later, as I checked out of the hotel, the manager greeted me warmly and handed me a bottle of expensive sake. "For our friendship," he said, bowing.

In return, I opened my suitcase and gave him my precious red shirt. "Just because," I told him. He bowed deeply as I slid into my taxi.

The taxi pulled away and I thought: If only life were made entirely of days like this.

Contrary to popular opinion, Philip Blazdell wasn't raised by wolves or savages. He grew up in London, England and was educated by reading and eavesdropping on the conversations of his elders. This perhaps explains his strange view of the world and often-inappropriate choice of footwear. Philip currently divides his time between Middle England (pretty much like Middle Earth minus the Orcs and Hobbits) and obscure little towns in Japan. He is currently obsessed with European countries beginning with 'A' (Albania, Armenia, and Andorra) and still drinks far too much, far too often. His web site is www.philipblazdell.com.

A Taste for the Classics

Kindly mind those teeth, would you?

By Ken Penland

In 2001, I finished a 300-plus hour restoration job on one of my prized wood-and-canvas Old Town canoes. I took it out for a short celebratory first paddle on the C&O canal at Angler's Inn, on the Maryland side of the Potomac River.

It was a beautiful cloudless day, and as I paddled, I felt relaxed and peaceful. I was, in truth, enjoying more than just the placid waters and natural scenery. Many of the people I encountered that morning asked me about my boat, and I proudly recalled my extensive and painstaking rebuilding effort.

It had been a long journey for the canoe and myself. I found it in Bath, Maine—derelict and exposed to the elements, resting on sawhorses with tattered remnants of rotted canvas dripping forlornly from the gunwales. I purchased it for three hundred and fifty dollars, and a day or so later I spent an equal figure acquiring a collection of essential repair supplies at the Old Town factory, where it had been constructed thirty-four years earlier.

Once the canoe was back in Maryland, I began a multi-month process of overhauling it. The canoe needed both ends rebuilt, the decks replaced, seats re-caned, all existing varnish stripped, all discoloured wood bleached, sanding that never seemed to end, and four new coats of expensive UV-inhibiting varnish. Oh yes— and there was even more sanding between each coat of varnish. Fortunately, no structural ribs needed replacement. All this before I even started to re-canvas it!

Re-canvassing sounds easy when you read about it. It isn't. Thousands of brass tack heads had to be driven flush with the wood hull, questionable planking replaced, and a canvas sling rigged and tightened to stretch the fabric before setting the hull inside. Next began the meticulous process of tacking the fabric to the tips of the ribs, using sharp brass tacks installed by hand along the gunwales. These small tacks were picked up by hand and installed one at a time. The tacks exhibited all the endearing qualities of angry crabs, just waiting to inflict discomfort on their would-be handlers. It was slow and tedious work. Just ask my "former" friend who helped me with the procedure.

Once the canvas had been attached and cut down, it still needed to be "torched" off, which involves burning the fuzz from the fabric's weave to make it smoother – all without lighting anything important on fire. Of course, I was working with dry wood, varnish, flammable cotton, and a propane torch with a flame burning at two thousand degrees Fahrenheit … no reason to be nervous!

After this process, I "filled" the delicately scorched canvas with a special gritty paste, which I rubbed in by hand and allowed to dry. This oil-based filler took five full weeks in early summer to completely harden. I reattached the keel, applied multiple coats of hull paint, reinstalled the outer gunwales and brass trim, and addressed a hundred or so other small details until my prized canoe absolutely gleamed! And then I waited for just the right day to re-launch—and that day was on the Potomac River. Everything I had put into it now seemed completely justified as the canoe glided gently along.

About a half kilometre from the takeout, I saw an adult beaver swimming about four metres off the end of my boat. The beaver appeared to be missing one eye. I was paddling solo but saw a jogger on the towpath. I stopped paddling, turned in my seat, and called out to him as he passed: "Hey, check out the beaver." The jogger nodded in response.

The beaver swam to a spot roughly a metre from my boat. He suddenly dove, and with a loud tail slap, disappeared. A few seconds later, I heard the horrific and unmistakable sound of teeth and claws being drawn across the bottom of my canoe.

"What the hell?" I yelled. Momentary shock washed over me. The jogger, who had been watching the beaver swim, said: "Oh, he's just playing with you!"

"Playing with me?" I cried. "He's chewing a hole in my boat!"

I rolled the hull from side to side, trying to shake the beaver free. The scratching noises stopped for a few seconds, but I soon felt him latch onto the boat's keel at the midsection. I shook the canoe even more violently. Then I reached over the side and tried poking him away from the boat with the blade of my wooden paddle. That dissuaded him briefly, but after a few seconds he returned and swam along the side of the boat, scratching at it.

That was the clincher. If he wanted to pick a fight, I would give him one. I aimed at his head and struck him hard with the edge of my paddle. This failed to impress the critter, and he came back for more. Each time he came within reach, I struck at him, over and over and over again.

Our fight—a 185-pound man versus a 45-pound demonically possessed beaver—went on for more than two minutes. It ended when the beaver broke off the engagement by surfacing just beyond my reach. He eyed me coldly with his one good orb as if to say, "And if you want more of that, just come back sometime!"

He swam away, and I hastily retreated towards the takeout.

On terra firma, I pulled the boat from the water, inverted it, and checked the damage. The beaver had scraped the paint all the way down to the canvas filler in ten places. He had punctured the new canvas below the waterline—along the stem of the boat—and he had bitten halfway through the solid ash keel, which was an inch and a half thick. Even my paddle had suffered a significant crack when I had used it to club him over the head.

I was so shocked by the encounter that I reported the incident to the C&O canal park managers. I showed my boat off at a local paddle shop with the water still dripping off the canoe's damaged parts; then I took pictures of the scrapes, scratches, and bite marks with a disposable camera.

Most people who have heard my tale of woe show genuine surprise and sympathy when I tell it. Only later, I suspect, do they slip away and laugh themselves silly.

I have since repaired the damage to my prized canoe, but if you look carefully, you can still see where the beaver dragged his incisors along the stem in an attempt to chomp through the boat. The new brass stem band probably saved it from extensive damage. If the canoe had been made of "modern" materials such as fiberglass, Kevlar, molded plastic, or aluminum, the beaver's teeth and claws would have done little harm.

Of all the boats that paddle on that body of water, perhaps only one in several hundred is wood-and-canvas. That beaver sure knew how to pick his target.

Ken Penland was trained as an environmental scientist and by his own admission suffers from a bad case of smallboatitis. This clinically undiagnosed condition leads those afflicted to collect and use various small watercraft for recreation, despite the pleas of friends and family. He is open to the idea of forming a "support group" for like-minded sufferers ... provided that it meets somewhere on the water. Penland has paddled the C&O canal in his wood-and-canvas canoe many times since the incident, and has never again encountered the psychotic beaver. He currently lives in Virginia.

Siren Eyes

When travelling with your husband greatly lowers your life expectancy.

By Leslie Bamford

The wind howled. The sailboat bucked and wallowed. As I clung to a rail in the sailboat's cockpit, the wind whipping hair into my eyes, I looked up at my husband Bob. His face was set in a grimace, his hands tightly gripping the wheel. The ice-cold water sprayed over us and the sailboat was heeled so far over that I thought it was going to turn belly up.

We were on vacation and I was about to die. Again.

"You have to experience sailing in the North Channel," Bob had said when we woke up that morning in our quaint Gore Bay motel. "Seeing the North Channel by boat is an absolute must if you want the real Manitoulin Island experience."

Needless to say, the trip was Bob's idea. He had started wearing me down in the winter while the snow was still covering the ground at home.

"Let's get back to nature," he had said. "What could be better for a summer holiday?"

His first choice was Manitoulin Island, land of Gitchi Manitou, the Great Spirit. Set between Lake Huron, Georgian Bay, and the

North Channel, Manitoulin (as Bob reminded me) is the largest freshwater island in the world.

"You'll love it," he said. "There's fabulous scenery, and we can visit before the bugs come out." He waved a pamphlet for the Chi-Cheemaun ferry in my direction, his blue eyes flashing with excitement.

I should have known those blue eyes were luring me, like Sirens, to my demise. Bob's enthusiasm for trying new things always seems to involve me and a life-threatening activity. But I never see it coming. So from the safety of our living room that January, I ignored the sinking feeling in the pit of my stomach and agreed to go.

*   *   *

After a week on the island, Bob's promise of beautiful scenery was still in question. Mind you, it was hard to see *anything* through the constant sleet and snow. But he was right about the bugs: there were none to be found on Manitoulin Island that June. It was too bloody cold. Mount Pinatubo in the Philippines had recently erupted, which unbeknownst to us had spread a haze of sulphuric acid into the earth's atmosphere, blocking the sun and lowering temperatures worldwide. We packed bathing suits and sunscreen, but spent the first week of our vacation wearing parkas and mitts to stay warm in the near-freezing weather. When it wasn't raining, it was snowing.

Lesson learned: never travel with a Siren-eyed man if a volcano has recently erupted.

The morning we went sailing, the sun had come out for the first time in a week. Throwing off our parkas and mitts, we donned shorts and T-shirts and went outside. It was still cool, but the June sun had warmth in it, and we eagerly walked around Gore Bay Harbour looking for an appropriate place to buy some breakfast.

"Let's charter a sailboat today," Bob said. "They sail right from here."

Before I could think of a suitable reply, Bob whisked me into the office of North Channel Charters. Sounds official enough, I thought—no doubt a professional organization that's out of our price range, and unlikely to charter a boat to the likes of us anyway.

The office was actually a shamble of boat parts, papers, charts, and ashtrays full of cigarette butts. Behind the counter, a pudgy man in denim overalls was talking on the phone. He waved to us and went on talking. After ten minutes he hung up and asked how he could help us.

"We want to charter one of your sailboats today," said Bob.

The man and Bob discussed boats and prices while I tried to find something in the office to feign interest in, without any luck.

"Will you be our captain?" I heard Bob asking the man.

"Sure will," he replied. "And you'll love the boat. She's a thirty-four-foot Catalina. Perfect for a sail in the channel. Come back at ten. We'll be out for about three hours, round trip."

Before I could object, the captain swiped Bob's Visa card and we were back outside in the sun. Bob was smiling from ear to ear.

"Let's go back to the lodge and put on our bathing suits," he said.

"Are we going swimming off the boat?"

"Hell, no! The water is barely above freezing—you'd probably die of hypothermia if you went swimming for even ten minutes. We'll sunbathe. On the boat."

The words "barely above freezing" and "die of hypothermia" stood out in my mind—the water sounded like a death trap waiting for its next victim. But I tried to focus on the boat. I like boats, at least conceptually. Not that I'd ever been on a large sailboat. Or any sailboat, for that matter. Just a Hobie Cat (a small two-hulled boat, or catamaran), on another vacation when Bob had tried to kill me.

"What should we take?" I asked. "Food? Jackets?"

"We'll only be gone for three hours and we just ate, so I don't think we'll need any food. I'm sure they'll supply snacks, anyway. And look at the weather. It's beautiful! Who needs a coat? Sunscreen is more appropriate. And maybe some sweatpants and a sweatshirt to put on over our bathing suits if it cools off later."

Lesson learned: never listen to a man with Siren eyes when there is sulphuric acid in the atmosphere.

Just before ten, we walked over to the office of North Channel Charters, which is when things took a turn for the worse.

"I won't be your skipper today after all," said the man in the overalls. "Something came up. My son is going to take you instead." He waved his hand toward a scruffy kid sitting at the end of the counter smoking a cigarette. The kid looked about twelve.

"Oh that's fine," said Bob, holding out his hand to the boy. "My name's Bob Bamford and this is my wife Leslie. And you are?"

"Mors."

"Pardon?"

"Mors."

When the man in overalls saw Bob's raised eyebrows at the boy's incomprehensible grunt, he intervened. "That's my son Maurice," he said. "Named him after Rocket Richard. Man, could that guy skate. Maurice got the name but not the speed. Likes to sit around way too much."

He looked at his son, then back at Bob. "Teenagers ... what are you going to do?"

He turned to Maurice, who was still sitting on the stool. "Time to go, son, while the weather holds. Chop, chop. And remember to be back in three hours."

We followed Mors as he shuffled in his flip-flops along the dock toward a large white boat. He wore creased beige shorts and a white T-shirt with stains on the front. A pack of cigarettes bulged out of one back pocket.

Once we were on board, Mors started the engine and instructed Bob on how to assist with the mooring lines so we could cast off. Soon we were motoring out of the harbour. The water was calm and the wind was light. I slathered myself with sunscreen and settled back on the cockpit cushions to soak up some much-anticipated rays. In the background I could hear Bob making conversation with Mors about raising the sails; each question of Bob's was inevitably followed by a two- or three-word answer from Mors.

Soon Mors turned off the motor and raised the sails. We were sailing.

Mors put the winch handles in their holders, then gathered up the excess lines and tossed them down the companionway in a heap.

Bob turned to me. "Not ship-shape, throwing the lines below like that," he whispered. "Be careful you don't trip on them."

"Why don't you just tell him?" I whispered back.

"He's the skipper," replied Bob. "He's in charge. Sailing etiquette, you know."

I didn't know, and I didn't particularly care. I was just happy that it was warm and peaceful. Water lapped against the boat. Finally I could relax.

Mors steered while Bob and I lay in the cockpit. After an hour I sat up and looked around. We were sailing in the middle of a large body of water, with land on both sides. I peered into the distance to see what kind of cottages people had around here. I didn't see any; both shorelines were undeveloped. There were no cottages, no docks, no other boats, no people. Not even a bear fishing off a rock. We were alone in the middle of nowhere.

"We're going to a place I've always wanted to see," Bob said, leaning toward me in the cockpit. "The Benjamin Islands. They're made of pink granite. Mors says we'll love them."

I found it hard to imagine Mors saying anything of the kind, but who was I to spoil the look of bliss on the face of a Siren?

"Are we there yet?" I asked, noting that we were just about halfway through our allotted time.

"Almost," said Mors.

At the end of our second hour we were still not there. But the sun was still shining and my Scottish nature enjoyed the fact that we were going to get more than our money's worth out of this charter.

The wind began to pick up just as some islands came into sight about half an hour later.

"The Benjamins!" Bob exclaimed. He was beaming. "See how narrow the channels are between them? We're going to sail right through those channels."

He waved a chart at me. "These islands are called Sow and Pigs and The Boar. Isn't that cute?"

Adorable, I thought as I smiled back at him.

"If you haven't run aground, then you haven't been to the Benjamins," offered Mors, a cigarette hanging out of his mouth.

"What?" I asked.

"It's an old saying in these parts. Don't worry, it's fine. I know how to navigate. There's a dangerous section coming up."

Bob and Mors took down the sails, and then Mors began to turn the wheel —first clockwise, then counterclockwise—as we motored between the rocks. Suddenly his expression darkened and he tossed his cigarette overboard.

"I'm not sure ..." he muttered.

Bob looked at the chart, looked at Mors, then looked at the chart again. "I think we should be further to starboard," Bob said.

"I don't know," said Mors again.

"Haven't you done this before?" Bob asked. His face was serious now.

"Never. I just turned eighteen. This is the first time my father sent me out on a charter."

I looked at Bob. He looked at me, then back to the chart. "Over to starboard, Mors. NOW!"

The boy turned the wheel. Rocks were visible just below the surface of the water. I held my breath as we maneuvered between huge granite shelves in the narrow channel.

"We made it," said Mors, who looked visibly shaken. He brought the boat around a couple of islands, then back out into open water through a wider channel. He and Bob raised the sails again.

"I'm going below now. You can sail the boat, Mister."

"Can you get us a snack from down there?" I asked.

"No food on board, ma'am."

"Oh, well, a cold drink then."

"No drinks, either."

Mors went below. We'd been out for four hours now. The sun had faded behind a bank of clouds and the wind was steadily picking up.

Within minutes, the sky was dark and the temperature had plummeted. The wind began to howl and the boat heeled over at a dangerous angle. I scrambled for our sweatshirts and sweatpants while Bob steered. Mors remained below, sitting at the table and smoking cigarettes. The wind off the frigid water blew right through our clothes and soon I was shivering from both fear and the cold.

We were in a dangerous environment with a novice who had never been out by himself, and we had no idea what we were doing.

The boat heeled over further as large waves began to rock the craft.

"The boat's falling over," I said to Bob as I hung onto the cockpit railing. "Make it stop."

"It's not falling over, it's heeling over," Bob said from his position at the wheel. "It won't tip. It's designed to do this. If you want to get back to Gore Bay today, we have to sail like this. I can't make it stop without sailing in the wrong direction."

"I'm scared," I said. I could feel panic rising in my stomach. "We're sinking, I know we are. We're going to fall out and drown. Or freeze to death in that water."

At that moment, several loud bangs echoed from below deck. Terrified, I looked down the companionway, expecting to see a hole in the bottom of the boat. Instead, I saw pots and pans skittering across the floor. Doors to various compartments were opening and closing. Mors sat at the table, smoking furiously, staring into the void.

Gingerly, with my head down to avoid flying objects, I went below and collected the pans, stowing them inside cupboards and making sure the latches were properly shut on all the doors. Mors wouldn't even look at me. The boat rocked and bucked, making it difficult to stand up. The lines Mors had thrown below earlier snaked around the floor, grabbing at my ankles, tripping me several times.

I was just getting the hang of avoiding the lines when my body was tossed from one side of the boat to the other and slammed hard against the bulkhead. As I attempted to reorient myself, I felt a sharp pain in my shoulder. My head could understand what had happened, but my stomach could not. Bile rose in my throat.

"I'm going to be sick!" I moaned.

Mors emitted a huge puff of smoke.

"SICK!" I yelled.

Mors pointed to a doorway. I opened it. A peculiar-looking contraption stared back at me, something that resembled a toilet, but different. I hesitated as I tried to imagine how it worked. Then I heard Bob calling, "Come back up. You'll get sick down there."

I looked at Mors again. He was chain-smoking, lighting a new cigarette from the old one. Apparently he had been blessed with a cast iron gut, but few other redeeming qualities.

I climbed back up into the cockpit, stumbling as my feet got caught in the lines again. The air hit me like a blast from the Arctic and I began to shiver again.

"Good work down there, stowing those pots," said Bob.

"Go to hell," I said.

"We'll be okay. I can do this."

"Have you ever sailed a boat like this?"

"Well no, but ..."

"Maybe I should just jump off and get it over with."

"Take the wheel."

"No bloody way."

Just then, a gust of wind came out of the sky like a giant hand, grabbing the Catalina and pushing her down. I saw the water coming up at us, saw the sail falling. I waited for the smash of the mast against the water. At the last second, the boat popped up like a cork, righting itself.

"What the hell was that?" I gasped.

"The wind almost knocked us down. But did you see what happened? It didn't." Bob gripped the wheel more tightly and focused. But I couldn't hear him. Or *wouldn't* hear him. Fear of death had intervened. I sat shivering, waiting for the next blow-down. The one that would be our last.

My thoughts raced. Who would have guessed I would meet my maker on the North Channel, land of Gitchi Manitou? Me, a big-city girl who never intended to have anything to do with nature. I was more of a five-star-resort-and-swimming-pool kind of gal.

I shivered, waited. Then I felt a presence, something beyond the sky, waiting along with me. Waiting for me? I knew that the only way to get to that presence was to die. And I knew I didn't want to die. Not today. Not ever, really.

"Take the wheel," Bob said. "It's the only way to stop being afraid."

I looked at Bob, hating him, hating boats, and hating wind and sails, and boys who smoked, and God. Especially God. For making us die to find Him.

"Please," said Bob. "I'll hold it with you. Just try it for a minute."

I forced myself to stand up and squeeze behind the wheel. I put my hands on the icy chrome and held on. Bob held it too. I felt something. A tension. A connection of some kind.

"I feel something," I said. "What is it?"

"It's the sail, the keel, and the angle of the wind," said Bob. "Now turn the wheel to port a little bit." I turned to the right. "No, port is left," said Bob, guiding my hands. "Feel that?" I turned to the left and felt the tension on the sail lessen. "Now keep it like that for a few minutes, but then you'll have to turn to starboard again to stay on course. The boat will heel over more. Try it."

I turned the wheel to the right and the tension came back. The boat leaned again, but this time I could feel the keel keeping her from tipping over. I could feel it through the wheel, through my hands, through my body. I could feel the safety of the boat's design, doing exactly what she was made to do.

I looked at Bob. He was sitting in the cockpit. I was sailing the boat.

After a while I stopped gripping the wheel like I was strangling it. I stopped shivering. I stopped hating Bob, hating boats, and hating God. I even stopped hating Mors.

I stayed at the helm for two hours until Gore Bay Harbour came back into view. Then Bob took over. Mors emerged from his sweat lodge below deck to help me take the sails down and direct Bob to the North Channel Charters dock.

Bob brought the Catalina into her slip like a pro, leaving Mors gaping in admiration, his tobacco-stained mouth open.

"I think Mors was terrified out there," Bob said under his breath as we tidied up the lines.

"His father should never have sent him out with so little experience," I said. "He could have run the boat aground."

"But he knew when to listen and he did what I said. Best of all, he let us sail the boat!"

"Spoken like a true Siren," I said.

"Huh?"

"Never mind."

"We ought to thank him," said Bob. "He needs to hear something positive before his father tears a strip off him for being gone seven hours instead of three."

"Just don't breathe in when you get close—he's probably still exhaling."

Before we clambered off the boat, Bob approached Mors and said, "Good job out there, buddy." He patted Mors on the shoulder and shook his hand.

"Bye, Mors," I said. "Thanks for everything." I offered my hand and held my breath. His grip was damp and limp, but he smiled at me for a second before turning and plodding toward the office and whatever retribution awaited him. I found myself hoping his father would go easy on him.

Bob turned to me. "Let's go, honey. I'm buying you a gigantic martini. To celebrate."

"To celebrate what? Another near-death experience?"

"All you needed was two minutes at the wheel and you were hooked on sailing. I saw your face. Come on, admit it!"

"That look was me giving God a piece of my mind," I said.

"Good place to encounter God, here in the land of Gitchi Manitou."

"Can we go somewhere less spiritual next year? Somewhere with a pool and a bar and no God? I'm thinking Vegas."

"I'm thinking a sailing trip down the inland waterway to Chesapeake Bay. You'll love it. I watched you today. You're a natural."

"You always say that after you nearly kill me."

"Let's talk about it over drinks."

"Right," I said, and I took Bob's hand in mine.

Leslie Bamford is happy to be alive after sixteen years of marriage to her adventurous husband. Bob's idea of a good time usually involves some sort of death-defying experience. This makes for good stories later, written in the safety of her home with a fat cat named Blackberry on her lap and occasional visits from her mother's ghost. When Leslie isn't recruiting volunteers for the municipal government, she is working on a book about her wacky life with Bob, which she hopes to finish before one of his vacation plans does her in. She lives in Waterloo, Ontario.

Things That Go Bump in the Outhouse

Sit down at your own peril.

By Zak Cross

"Uh, Zak, I think there's something in the outhouse," stuttered Johnny, who looked a few shades paler than when I'd last seen him.

I have to admit, during the seven years I've been leading trips for youth into the wilderness, I've never heard those exact words. Being the fearless leader of this group of teenage boys, I took it upon myself to investigate.

The outhouse was only about ten metres away, so I strolled up the path toward it, wondering what strange noise could have upset Johnny so much. Standing in front of the outhouse, I reached forward and gingerly pushed the door. As it squeaked open, it revealed nothing. The outhouse was empty. The only thing out of place was a smear of feces on the toilet seat. I made a mental note to mention the benefits of cleanliness to Johnny, but then felt compelled to look further.

Had he actually meant *in* the outhouse? I entered and slowly peered over the edge of the seat. At that very moment a flash of fur passed through a faint shaft of light beneath me. I jumped back out of the small structure and the door slammed shut.

"Holy Crap! There's something *in* the outhouse," I said out loud. I had no idea what it could be. It looked vaguely like a fox, but it couldn't really be a fox—could it?

With renewed confidence, I reached out and once again pushed the door open, then slowly crept forward and convinced myself to look down into the hole again. A narrow beam of light penetrated the darkness, and as my gaze settled, not six feet below me the head of a cougar moved into the light. A split second later our eyes locked, and the feline's lips drew back into a snarl.

I stumbled backwards, then ran from the outhouse. At the same moment I heard a terrible *crunch!* as the cat's head hit the underside of the seat platform. It had obviously jumped for the opening.

With my head still reeling, I called the group of boys together for an emergency meeting. I explained what had happened and asked them what they thought we should do. I wanted to listen to their ideas before making a decision. As we talked, we could hear the cat making repeated attempts to get free from its gruesome prison. It was decided that, even though it was nightfall, we would break camp and paddle our canoes by moonlight to another location.

Much later, after we had again established a campsite and settled in for the night, I had the chance to sit down with Johnny and hear what had actually happened to him. It turns out he had been standing in the outhouse doing his business when, out of the darkness, a set of claws appeared and took a swipe at his private parts. I found out later that at least two other boys had visited the outhouse before Johnny; one of them had sat down to do his business, which surely explained the smear on the toilet seat.

The next day, we contacted BC Parks officials, who went to the site and found a juvenile (two- or three-year-old) cougar at the bottom of the outhouse, nearly dead. They believed the young cat had become separated from its mother and was unable to hunt on its own, for it was near starvation.

No one will ever know how that young cougar found his way into such a gruesome predicament, but I can tell you one thing: whenever I visit an outhouse, I now look twice before sitting down.

Zak Cross has recently cut his hair and is thinking about cutting the lawn next. He lives on Vancouver Island with his family and a dog named Harper, who votes green.

The Fall Guy

Macho is as macho does. Unfortunately.

By Philip Torrens

We were lounging 'round the restaurant table after dinner: me, my buddy Graham, and Sue, the woman I'd been dating for a couple of months. It had become obvious that Graham was also attracted to Sue. As rivals, he and I were pretty evenly matched: We were both bearded, bespectacled, bookish geeks. But Graham was a geek with a pilot's license. He was also a master parachute jumper.

Parachuting was one pursuit we'd never pursued together. The first time he'd suggested it, I'd confided in him that I'm terrified of heights; I get vertigo using a footstool to retrieve a can of soup from the top shelf. So it was clearly no accident when, with studied casualness, he sprung the trap in the guise of a friendly invitation: "I should take you and Sue skydiving sometime."

"I've always wanted to try that!" Sue enthused, practically jumping out of her seat. As though we were on opposite ends of an invisible seesaw, I slumped down as she rose up. Hiding under the table suddenly looked like an attractive proposition. But I couldn't lose face in front of Sue. While my frontal lobes screamed "No! No!" inside my head, I heard myself say, "Sounds like fun" in what I hoped was my best baritone growl—though it probably came out as a falsetto squeak.

That was how the three of us came to be winging our way in a rented plane to a jump school in the countryside. It being January, the school was offering a two-for-one off-season special for lessons and your first jump. Apparently, not a lot of folks want to leave perfectly serviceable airplanes in the middle of winter. Smart folks, those. Still, the bargain rate appealed to my thrifty nature as a way to beat the high cost of living. Or dying, as I was convinced the case would be.

After an uneventful flight, Graham landed us at the private strip next to the jump school, which was housed in a converted barn. A real estate agent would have described this building as "rustic." A realist would have described it as "wrecked." Weather and neglect had warped the board walls into picket fences. Through the resulting gaps, the winter wind whistled an Aeolian dirge and drove snowdrifts into the interior.

Though there were several other experienced parachutists there to jump with Graham, it turned out Sue and I were the only students. After signing our lives away on liability release forms, we were taken to a mock-up of an airplane fuselage. Constructed of two-by-fours and plywood nailed haphazardly to the inside wall, it looked less like an airplane than a treehouse knocked together by a cross-eyed and carpentry challenged child. We practised sitting in its doorway, legs curled beneath the underside, and pushing off into the "void." (Or such void as we could imagine in the few feet between the "plane" and the old bales of hay stacked below.)

Next, we practised the bent-legged roll, which is used to absorb the impact from a parachute landing. We did this by leaping from ever-greater heights off a custom-made device that had been precisely engineered to generate forces equal to those we would actually encounter in the real situation. It was a good thing the instructor explained what a specialized piece of equipment it was—otherwise I would certainly have mistaken it for an ordinary stepladder.

In the afternoon, we were taken to the second floor of the barn. There, we were confronted by several rows of body harnesses hanging from the rafters. It resembled the sort of room one finds in the back of the more bizarre niche-market bars. (Or so I've heard.) We were there to hang in harnesses and rehearse the proper procedures in case of a parachute malfunction. If the main chute failed to open at all, we were to yank on the ripcord of our backup chute. But if the main chute opened but failed to deploy properly, we had to cut it away before opening the backup, lest the two chutes wrap and tangle together. Or maybe it was the other way around.

"But don't worry," the instructor assured us. In the event of a problem, we'd have a full seventeen seconds to realize something was wrong, diagnose the type of failure, determine the correct course of action, and take it, before we were too low for the handkerchief-sized backup chute to slow our fall sufficiently. No pressure.

Throughout the training, the wind had been blowing steadily. While Graham and the gang had been parachuting for hours, the instructor had been apologetically warning us it might be too turbulent for beginners to jump that day. I did my best to fake enormous disappointment at that prospect, though I'm not sure Sue was convinced by the act.

Then, as so often happens, the wind dropped just before dusk. We were hastily strapped into real parachutes and rushed to the jump plane, along with several seasoned skydivers determined to get in one final plunge.

The jump plane was a remarkable antique. It was now clear that the unlikely looking wooden mock-up in the barn had in fact been alarmingly accurate. The school owner's great, great grandfather must have bought this prototype cheap off the Wright brothers—and they must have used *that* money to build their first *real* airplane. It was the ultimate no-frills flying machine. They had dispensed with all luxuries. Like doors, for example. And really, who needs a door when it might just bang around in the slipstream once opened in flight? And you've got a parachute anyway, right?

The long ascent seemed to take forever, but paradoxically, not nearly long enough. As we approached jumping altitude, the jumpmaster leaned over to make sure my static line was clipped on. (A static line is a tear-away rope several yards long, attached to both the plane and the top of a jumper's parachute, so the chute's ripcord is automatically pulled out after they drop clear of the airplane. It's a precaution used with all first-time solo jumpers. Just in case, for example, they became so distracted by an especially lovely cloud, or by the novelty of bird watching from above, that it slips their mind that terra firma is approaching rather quickly.)

We finally straightened out from our spiralling climb, and the jumpmaster tossed out a weighted paper streamer. This was to gauge the wind drift so we would exit the plane at the right place in order to land within staggering distance of the barn. We circled around, and then straightened again.

"Jump run!" the jumpmaster announced; "Prepare to die!" was how I heard it.

Because of the tiny plane's low interior, we jumpers had been stacked like bobsled riders, each sitting between the legs of the one behind. I was at the head of the line, one leg already hooked out the doorway and beneath the plane. If I didn't jump, no one else could squeeze by me to go.

"Jump! Jump! Jump!" came the command.

A glance over my shoulder at the eager, expectant faces behind made it clear I would be deplaning very shortly, voluntarily or not. Reckoning I'd have a marginally better chance of surviving if I wasn't addled by a helpful boot to the head, I jumped. Or, more precisely, fell.

In theory, I was to face forward into the plane's slipstream, thrust myself fearlessly off, then assume the arch position— belly down, arms and legs lifted behind me, at one with the air, a modern-day Icarus. (Though perhaps that's not the happiest comparison, given what happened to Wax Wings Junior.) In fact, I was so terrified it took all my nerve to simply topple headfirst out of the doorway, not unlike a puppet whose strings had been suddenly snipped.

I did remember to face vaguely forward. This was nearly my undoing. The slipstream snatched my downward-pointing head and whipped it back between my legs as though I were a yogi attempting to achieve an impossible intimacy with myself. As I somersaulted repeatedly through the air, the static line wrapped itself over my shoulder and through my crotch. I reached the end of my tether and was then spun into a series of reverse somersaults as the static line unwound around me like a yo-yo string. There was a final sharp jerk, and I was drifting free.

Certain my inadvertent acrobatics must have fouled the chute's deployment, I peered apprehensively upward. No matter how old I live to be, I shall never achieve a sense of greater elation than I felt at seeing that properly filled white parachute spread wide and wonderful. I felt like a death row inmate receiving a last-minute pardon.

I spent a few peaceful moments drifting in the darkling sky, admiring the checkered fields far below. Then the tiny radio clipped to my shoulder crackled to life. It was there so that a controller on the ground, watching with binoculars, could direct me to pull down my left or right parachute toggle, spilling air to steer me away from ponds, power lines, and similar snares. By design, I could hear the controller but he couldn't hear me. I'm not sure whether this was because one-way radios are cheaper, or because over the years he had simply grown weary of listening to all the begging and blubbering from cowards like me.

Distracted by the steering directions, I didn't notice how quickly the ground was sneaking up. Rather than alighting gently, like a feather falling to earth, I slammed sideways into a ploughed field with all the grace of a stack of bricks pushed off the back of a speeding pickup truck.

As I sprawled there bruised and winded, Sue came down a few yards away. Naturally, she had jumped flawlessly and without fear. She also landed in textbook fashion with a beautifully executed roll, and then lay on her back in an ecstatic afterglow, red-cheeked with exhilaration, grinning infuriatingly.

Just then, a kindly gust snatched her chute, which she had neglected to collapse. (I had pulled down my own chute immediately after landing—the one thing I'd done right all day.) She was towed across the frozen furrows like a movie cowboy being dragged behind his horse. After ricocheting off icy clods of earth and pinballing off a few fenceposts, she was raked across fallen barbed wire as a finale. Her jump helmet protected her from serious injury, but she was roughed up enough that I felt karmic balance had been restored to the universe.

The only further misadventure that day was that our rented plane refused to start for our flight back to the city. We wound up bumming a lift with one of the other experienced jumpers who was driving our way. Our benefactor's ridiculously chiselled features were complimented by some impossibly macho name—Dirk Manhood, I think it was. With Graham and I jammed into the back seat of Dirk's Volkswagen Beetle, Sue sat up front, listening with starry eyes to tales of his aerial exploits.

It had been a tough and sometimes terrifying day, but I had survived my first—and last—parachute jump. More important, I hadn't wimped out in front of Sue, so it was all worth it. Or at least it was until she dumped me two weeks later. For Dirk.

Since the events described in this story, Philip Torrens has only flown in planes with fully pressurized cabins. Although he's never parachuted again, that hasn't stopped him from doing other silly things in an effort to impress the ladies. His misadventures have been published in several anthologies and outdoor magazines.

Skiing with Dad

And other reasons not to get out of bed in the morning.

By Sarah Bonar

Some of my favourite (and most embarrassing) memories of my dad are of the year he upgraded his downhill skis to extra-long slalom racing skis. I have now had fifteen years to recover from my teenage mortification, and my dad has had time to heal as well—physically, if not mentally.

Every year, our family bought downhill ski passes to our local resort. Downhill skiing was one of my dad's favourite activities. A self-professed adrenaline junkie (or suicide risk, depending on your point of view), he could often be spotted flying at terminal velocity down any number of ski runs, on the verge of losing control.

One year in particular stands out: The Year of the Slalom Skis.

To appreciate my experience, you have to understand that as a teenager growing up in a ski town, one's social status depended on what happened on the ski hill—and on what you wore. Everything had to be name-brand and colour-coordinated. This was the pre-snowboarding era, so the pinnacle of style was a Sun Ice pullover ski jacket (the double side zips were preferable to the single), paired with new name-brand gloves and a matching headband that covered your ears. The headband was more of an accessory than a necessity, as you would spend hours working it into your hair so that it "naturally" blended and accented your looks.

As well, your ski equipment had to be no more than two years old, and had to have some sort of extreme quality to it—ideally being promoted by the most extreme skiers on Warren Miller movies or in the ski magazines.

But all the thought and effort I put into my ski season could so easily be compromised by clueless family members—for example, my dad.

To be spotted with any family members during the day was a social killer, and they were to be avoided at all costs. Before one had a driver's license, parents were merely chauffeurs to and from the ski hill. And after receiving one's driver's license, parents were nothing but an annoyance.

Every situation encountered before, during, and after skiing was loaded with innuendo: who you sat with on the chairlift, who you were seen getting off the chairlift with, and which runs you went down. There were also subtle judgments based on which jumps you took, how you performed your jumps, when you went for lunch, and who you met at the ski lodge. All of these choices and actions could damage your status if you had not executed them carefully and correctly.

The driving force behind all this stress could be summed up with one word: Boys.

There always seemed to be a generous supply of cute boys on the hill. We mostly settled for skiing with guys in our own grade, which was fine, but we often fantasized about skiing with older boys in grades eleven and twelve, who we hoped would be watching for us.

My father, in my teenaged opinion, was the *antithesis* of everything cool. He wore the same boring ski outfit year after year, including an endless supply of goofy looking "practical" toques, one of which looked like a Russian hat lined with fur. But most of all, I was embarrassed by his clueless, impulsive actions. In my cool, perfectly orchestrated world, I was convinced that he deliberately set out to embarrass me. But I couldn't be entirely certain.

One day my friend Shari and I were skiing underneath the chairlift looking for a couple of cute older guys we had spotted earlier. We hoped they would bump into us on a run, but after a few hours of searching, we were still empty handed.

Then we saw them riding a chairlift, so we skied to the bottom and waited, trying to gauge how long it would take them to ski down the hill and get in line for the chair again. We would have to time it perfectly. If all went according to plan, we would spot them on their way past and slide in right behind them on the last ski run without looking like the stalkers we really were. Then we would stand in line right behind them for fifteen or twenty minutes and, if everything went according to plan, a conversation would ensue. If we were able to pull this off, we would have the most amazing ski day of our lives with the cutest boys on the hill!

As we waited patiently at the top of the last ski run, we saw them ski past. We followed. They slid into the line and, smoothly enough, so did we. This was it! It was the moment we had been waiting for all morning, if not our entire teenaged lives.

Just as I felt sure they were about to turn and talk to us, my dad cut into the line right behind us.

To my utter horror, he was covered from toque to boots with snow, apparently due to a recent wipeout. There were snowballs crusted in his toque and mustache, and snow lodged in his ears and goggles. There was snow inside his jacket, which he pulled open and shook violently. All the while, his torn and stained long-john top and ancient scarf were exposed for all to see.

I froze with horror and tried desperately to figure out how to diffuse this ticking bomb. My dad had definitely caught the attention of everyone in the immediate area, including those drop-dead gorgeous guys in front of us.

Then it happened—the point of no return. My dad "torpedoed" onto the back of one of the cute guys' skis.

For those of you not familiar with this terminology, "torpedoing" means that he blocked one nostril with his finger, then blew all the mucus out of the opposite nostril.

Shari and I looked at each other in utter disbelief. We then turned to watch the cute guy scrape up some snow with the back edge of his ski and, with an expression of obvious disgust, push off the offending glob. Mortified, I mumbled something about going for lunch and we hastily retreated out of line, knowing that today was not going to be the best day of our skiing career after all. Instead of wishing that these beautiful boys would remember us for the rest of their lives, we hoped we would never see them again.

This was just one in a series of incidents that reinforced the rule about never coming into contact with your parents on the ski hill. Even indirect contact could be fatal.

Another incident, almost equally embarrassing, occurred a week after my Dad upgraded his conventional downhill skis to slalom racing skis. Conventional skis have a lot more flexibility—and are thus more forgiving if a skier makes a mistake—than a stiff pair of racing skis.

In any case, Shari and I were riding the chairlift above a run known at that time as the Buckhorn. It was an intermediate run, so you only had to be at a moderate skiing level to ride it, and it was a lot of fun to cruise down at top speed, flying over the "rollers." (Rollers are arcing hills followed by shallow drops that you can catch air from if you ski fast enough.)

As we sat on the chair lift, hanging above the crest of one of the high rollers, I spotted my dad. He was standing at the top, catching his breath before engaging in the series of rollers that lay before him.

I turned to Shari and said, "There's my dad. He's going to see us, yell something embarrassing, then ski down over the rollers and wipe out." We laughed, watched, and waited.

Right on cue, my Dad saw us. He waved and yelled at us, getting everyone's attention on the chair lift and the ski hill around him. I pretended it wasn't me he was calling to.

Then he started his decent, accelerating toward the first roller in a tuck position. "YEEE-HAWWW!" he shouted as he hit the first roller. He lost his balance and shot up into the air at an odd angle, his right leg extending awkwardly out to counterbalance the rotation of his body. He descended below our line of view, but within seconds we saw an explosion of snow from behind the hill.

While the rest of the people on the lift probably worried about my dad's wellbeing, Shari and I laughed at how well I had predicted his stunt. As it turned out, he had broken two ribs and had to be tobogganed off the hill by the ski patrol.

If there was one thing I could credit my dad with, it was his persistence in trying to work those new racing skis. Even after his crash on the Buckhorn, he continued to use them. Early one morning, shortly after the ski hill had opened, he said, "Come on Sarah, let's go and do a run together."

Now, those who know my father understand that when he suggests something like this, it's not really a suggestion at all. You pretty much have to go along with all his suggestions because he shows such unbridled enthusiasm and would be greatly disappointed if you said no. So against my better judgment, and breaking that cardinal rule about being seen with one's parents, I agreed.

When we got to the top of the hill, I suggested to my dad that we try a run called Stem Winder.

The thing about Stem Winder is that it's a "tight" run; it's not very wide and it has a huge drop in the middle. During the course of a ski season, the flat section after the drop can become quite bumpy, so you have to absorb the bumps with your knees to prevent yourself from getting catapulted into the air. I thought my dad knew this.

We approached the top of the drop-off and stopped. I went first, cleared the drop, and coasted easily out onto the flats, even though the bumps were larger than normal. I had an uneasy feeling as I waited for my dad at the side.

My dad dropped over the edge, accumulated lots of speed, and was wildly out of control by the time he reached the bumpy flats. I watched him launch into the air and fly along parallel to the ground before landing hard on his back.

Just then, I noticed two cute boys appear above the drop-off. My dad was flopping around on the snow like a fish out of water—the wind had been knocked out of him. Flushed with embarrassment, I tried to look as cool as I could in such a circumstance.

"Dad, are you all right?" I asked as nonchalantly as possible. There was no response from my dad, just more rolling around.

I looked up and saw that the cute boys were intently watching my father. I wanted to die, but I figured I couldn't just leave him. Not yet, anyway.

After what seemed like an eternity, the cute boys at the top decided they had waited long enough. They started their descent, skillfully maneuvering around my dad, who was by this time pulling it together. As they zipped past him he raised his arm, shook his fist, and yelled, "What the HELL?!"

When there was no one in sight, I skied up to my dad to make sure he was okay. He was really pissed off, both at the "stupid run" and at "those little bastards" that nearly ran him over. When my dad gets mad, it is smart not to engage in any conversation, as his anger will gradually become focused on you. He was intent on going into the ski lodge, so I left him at the top of the final run, deciding to find some friends fast.

At the end of the day, I met my mom at the lodge. I figured we were going to wait for my father to finish his last run, but instead my mom said, "Sarah, we have to pick your dad up at the First Aid hut. Apparently he had a bad fall today."

As it turned out, my dad had actually knocked himself out on Stem Winder; he had no memory of his fall, or of the rest of the run down to the ski lodge. I think that was one of the last times he used those racing skis.

Sarah Bonar grew up in Cranbrook, BC where she participated in hiking, biking, skiing, and fishing trips with her dad. Sarah now has a child of her own, and she hopes that he'll grow up to recognize his mother's superior fashion sense, both on and off the slopes. These days, she looks forward to visits with her dad, even in public.

Somewhere West of Watson Lake

It can be a long, slow road to freedom.

By Paul McKinnon

God, I hate hitchhiking.

My friend Chuck and I had been on the road for five days. We had taken a city transit bus from downtown Vancouver to Horseshoe Bay, and stuck out our thumbs on the Trans-Canada Highway, heading east. Our destination? The Land of the Midnight Sun—Dawson City, Yukon.

We had planned to make it north in time for the summer solstice, which is not only the longest day of the year, but the date of a notorious ad hoc celebration in Dawson. Or so I had been told. I had never actually been to the Yukon, but Chuck had been up a couple of years before, and insisted on dragging me along this time.

"The solstice parties in Dawson are legendary," he told me. "The sun never sets, so people can't sleep and they all go crazy. We gotta get there for the solstice, man. We just gotta!"

But Chuck's plans have a tendency to change, and not always for the better. In this case, we had trouble achieving escape velocity in Vancouver. Not only does Chuck rarely have money (actually, he never has any money), but he'd left his tent and camping gear in a locker at the bus depot a couple of days too long. The Powers That Be had moved his gear and wouldn't give any of it back until he had forked over the cost of storage, which he didn't have. So we ended up sharing my one-man tent, and our friendship soon started feeling a little cramped.

After escaping Vancouver, we actually started making good time ... until we hit the Cassiar Highway in northern British Columbia. We ended up spending the solstice drinking cheap wine at the side of the dirt road just outside Dease Lake, nowhere near the Midnight Sun.

Did I mention that one of Chuck's other plans was to return to Dawson so that he could finish writing a novel?

"It's a great place to write because there are so many stories up north," he told me enthusiastically. "Everybody has a story, so you just steal them all and use them for the book. You should try it."

Part of what Chuck told me is true: almost everyone in the Yukon does have a story to tell. But what Chuck didn't tell me is that there are so many distractions that you can't get any writing done—you're too busy living your own story. Or series of stories.

And the longer we were on the road, the more stories we lived. Like the guy who picked us up in a brand new sports car that he had just bought in Vancouver. He wanted to see how fast it would go, and by the time the radar detector kicked in, the police had already passed us going the other way. They turned around and eventually caught up with us. Our driver was awarded a hefty ticket for speeding, but as soon as the cops were out of sight, he stomped on the gas pedal and we blasted down the road like buckshot from a twelve-gauge. We made good time that day, thanks to our lead-footed driver.

But the best was yet to come.

"It'll be great," Chuck enthused. "We'll be like Robert Service and Jack London, only bigger. I'll be the new Robert Service, and you can be the new Jack London."

I told Chuck that *I* wanted to be the new Robert Service, and *he* could be the new Jack London. We both knew that Jack London had left the Yukon because he caught scurvy, and that he had died of an overdose of morphine when he was forty.

We decided that we'd both be the new Robert Service, and to hell with Jack London. What did he know?

By the time Chuck and I reached the Yukon border, we were both sick of hitchhiking and sick of each other. We hadn't showered since Vancouver. The tent seemed to get smaller and stinkier each night.

We looked at the map. Dawson City was a six-hour drive north of Whitehorse, and Whitehorse was still several hours away. What had we been thinking?

"Well," said Chuck, "at least we're on the Alaska Highway now. There's a lot more traffic along here."

That was true. The Cassiar Highway had certainly been a bad stretch of road. And there *were* a lot more vehicles driving the

Alaska Highway. The only trouble was that most of them were recreational vehicles—massive motor homes filled with retirees. And they weren't stopping for anyone. These people no doubt believed that all hitchhikers were psychopathic killers waiting like wolves at the side of the road. We knew they had plenty of room in their RV leviathans, and that just made me more resentful. Most of them wouldn't even wave. The bastards!

We found ourselves stranded somewhere west of Watson Lake.

"If only we could get to Whitehorse," I groaned. "I know someone in Whitehorse. She'll feed us and bathe us. She'll lend us money. Maybe she'll even drive us to Dawson City." I just knew she would.

Back in Vancouver, Chuck and I had made a sign for our travels. Using a black felt pen, we had written on a piece of dirty cardboard:

ANYWHERE BUT HERE!

It had seemed humorous at the time. But not anymore.

The morning of our fifth day on the road, I finally snapped.

"Gimme that sign!" I barked at Chuck. I flipped it over and scrawled a new message on the back:

RVs SUCK!

"That's not going to help," Chuck said.

"They're not stopping anyway!" I yelled. "What's the difference?"

"They'll stop," Chuck assured me. "One of them will stop eventually."

"Eventually?" I screamed. "We've been hitchhiking for five days and we aren't even in Whitehorse yet! By the time we get to Dawson the summer will be over!"

As we argued, another RV passed us. That was it. I couldn't hack it anymore. I dropped my pants and mooned them.

"Here's something for your rear-view mirror, you jerk!"

A mosquito bit me on the butt.

"Serves you right," said Chuck, laughing.

I started toward him with intentions of murder ... and then it happened. Suddenly we were covered in a cloud of smoke and noise. When the dust settled, there was an enormous tour bus idling by the side of the road. The door opened, and Chuck and I peered inside. A huge black man was sitting behind the wheel.

"Where y'all headed?" he drawled in a thick American accent.

"Dawson City!" we said.

"Well ... I'm only going as far as Whitehorse," he replied. "But if you want a lift, hop on board."

We hopped on board pretty damn quickly.

The bus was empty. It had broken down in Watson Lake two days before, and the tour company had sent another bus down from Whitehorse to pick up the passengers. Now the driver was behind the wheel of an empty bus heading to Whitehorse, and he wanted a little company for the ride north. Chuck and I couldn't believe our good luck.

Our driver's name was Andrew Boyd. He was from Oklahoma, and he *hated* driving the Alaska Highway during the summer. Too many damn RVs along the route slowing him down. He passed all of them.

Chuck and I just stared out the windows, smiling at all the motor homes as we whizzed by.

I made another sign:

EAT MY DUST!

After our excruciatingly slow start, we covered the final distance to Whitehorse in record time. My friend was in town, and I somehow managed to track her down. Two days later, we arrived in Dawson City in an RV piloted by three young guys from Austria. When we got into Dawson, Chuck and I bought them a drink.

Dawson City was everything Chuck had promised, even if we did miss the solstice. It was one of the best summers I've ever had.

God, I love hitchhiking.

Paul McKinnon lives in Victoria, British Columbia, where he writes and performs for the comedy troupe The 30 Cent Players. To see some of his video work online go to YouTube and type 30centplayers (all one word) into their search engine. To contact Paul please email him at mcsquare@shaw.ca.

Fantasy Island

Some fantasies are worth their weight in rat droppings.

By Ron Johnson

U pon arrival in Chichiriviche, a seaside town about three hours west of Caracas, Venezuela, I set out to fulfill one of my lifelong fantasies.

My dream was to spend a delightful night on a secluded and deserted island with my girlfriend Yvette. She was as excited about the getaway as I was. We had been going together for several months in Venezuela and we felt it was time to take a break from the noise and commotion of the big city.

Originally from Trinidad, Yvette now made Venezuela her home, but she had never ventured to this part of the country before. Still, as we stood on the beach looking at the islands offshore, it was readily apparent that most of them received heavy use. With no desire to join swarms of other tourists, I peered out over the Caribbean searching for another option. There, far to the north, I saw a speck on the horizon. I asked a local fisherman what the name of that island was.

"Cayo Borracho. Usted no quiere ir alli."

Of course, telling me that I didn't want to go there aroused my curiosity.

"Por que?" I asked.

A torrent of indecipherable Spanish erupted from the fisherman's lips.

It has been noted that I have a bad habit of nodding my head in agreement even when I don't understand everything that's been said. Here, I did it again. The fisherman spoke too fast for me to understand, and my pride prevented me from asking further questions. We would soon find out exactly what he had said.

We purchased food and water for two days and struck a deal for transport to Cayo Borracho, which in English means simply, "Drunk Island." Exuberant, we set forth with the fisherman in his small skiff, and three hours later we set foot on our tropical isle. The few words I *had* understood from the fisherman had been right: the water *was* rough, and yes, it *was* a long way to the mainland. With a look of uncertainty, our captain promised to return the next day, weather permitting. Then he departed, leaving us to fend for ourselves.

Fantasy Island! Here I stood at last, alone with my girlfriend, and no one to disturb the solitude. We quickly shed our clothes and took to the water with snorkels and fins to explore the beautiful coral that ran adjacent to the shoreline. Engulfed in this underwater paradise, I ventured away from the shore (and my partner), entranced by the multitude of colorful fish as they flitted in all directions.

That's when I saw something on the bottom curled beneath a piece of coral. It appeared to be an eel. As I ventured closer the water became quite shallow, and I did not need to dive much further for a better look.

A previous visit to the underwater aquarium in Curacao had educated me on many forms of aquatic life, so what I saw in that coral caused me immediate alarm. This was no eel, but the dreaded sea snake!

The highly venomous serpent took exception to my intrusion and came forth to greet me. I performed an about-face and with flippers in full gear, splashed my way toward the now-distant shoreline, expecting at any moment to receive a lethal dose of venom. Fear, that great protector, propelled me like never before, and in no time I pulled myself onto the beach. The snake, I noted thankfully, had given up the chase.

Back on land, I discovered that I couldn't walk. My legs had cramped up severely from heavy exertion, and it would be some time before I rid myself of the excruciating pain in my calves. This put a damper on any further underwater exploration; besides, I was not about to contest the snake's domain anymore.

"That was a close call," I said to Yvette. "Obviously, no one ever comes out here. Those snakes don't like visitors."

"Well, maybe it's time we set up camp and have a bite to eat," she replied. "How about we leave the water life alone? I wasn't too comfortable out there myself, especially after you took off for the horizon."

We hung our single hammock between two windblown palms, made a snack, and fought the unremitting wind in our attempt to organize our modest campsite. We then made our way to the beach, au natural, to relax and take in the sun. After the earlier excitement, I was now eager to relax and I allowed myself to drift into a meditative state. With the wind caressing my body and fondling my hair, I was soon lulled into a state of peace that is difficult to attain in the presence of other people.

"Hola."

Startled, I came out of my reverie and saw a young man approaching us from about thirty metres away. Too late now for modesty, I simply responded, "Hola."

Yvette was too shocked to do anything but stare at him.

"Where did you come from?" I asked.

"I'm camped on the other side of the island," he said, sitting down on the sand beside us. He seemed completely oblivious to our non-attire. "My name is Franco. I heard your boat come in a while ago, so I thought I'd drop over and see who'd joined me out here."

Still quite stunned by this intrusion, I asked Franco how long he'd been out here.

"I've been here for a week already. It's been remarkable! I'm from France, and I wanted to see what being alone on an island would be like."

"Well, sorry we disturbed you. We're looking for the same thing."

"No problem, this island is big enough for all of us." Franco pointed to the southeast. "My camp is over there, in the far corner. There's less wind."

We made small talk for about an hour, and then Franco returned to his side of the island, leaving us once more in privacy. The lonely planet does not seem to be very lonely anymore, even on supposedly deserted islands. Although his intrusion had upset the tranquility, I was determined not to let it undermine the purpose of this retreat—our serene and romantic getaway.

Unfortunately, venomous snakes and people have a way of disturbing my serenity.

As the sun slowly ebbed in the western sky, so did my anxiety—until I spotted a sudden movement on the beach.

"Did you see that?" I asked Yvette.

"Yes," she said, "but I don't know what it is. It's getting dark."

I returned to the campsite and retrieved my flashlight, then pointed the beam into the darkness, scanning the beach for movement. There! A pair of red eyes!

Now the fisherman's earlier reference to "ratons" became clear. It was a rat. And not just one—several were now scurrying across the sand. One of them was brave enough to scurry right up to my foot before I shooed him away. Rats were the last things I had expected this many miles from the mainland, and as darkness settled in, more and more of the beasts appeared from the shadows.

We returned to our campsite and discovered that the vermin had taken over. Like a scene from the movie *Ratatouille*, they were attempting to get into our food and scampering all around us. To stop them from doing so, we hurriedly gathered everything and hoisted our food into a tree. The howling wind only added to the turmoil.

Finally, with no other options but to let the rodents reign, we attempted a feat bordering on the impossible—two persons sleeping in one hammock. Neither of us wanted to sleep on the rodent-infested beach with the blankets we had brought. After much repositioning, it appeared that sleep might actually be possible. With the wind blowing the hammock back and forth, we felt ourselves being rocked to sleep.

And then I felt teeth sinking into my backside.

"Ouch!" I screamed.

"What?" asked a startled Yvette.

"I just got bit in the rear by one of those rats. We can't stay like this. We'll have to see if we can get the hammock higher in the trees."

In the darkness, with the furry creatures running over our feet, we managed to raise the hammock to an elevation that prevented further attacks. Sleep, regrettably, was not fast in coming. Nor was the dawn.

When the fisherman came for us the next day, we were very happy to see him. Bidding farewell to our "tropical paradise" was not difficult. We concluded that to stay on Cayo Borracho, the "Drunk Island," one probably had to be inebriated.

So much for my island fantasy.

Ron Johnson has since upgraded his hammock for vacations at Caribbean all-inclusive resorts. He has concluded that the only place he'll find that idyllic paradise is in fiction. Watch for more of his Venezuelan exploits in his upcoming book, Hooked on a Drumbeat. *Its publication date will be announced shortly on his web site,* **www.drumbeats06.com**.

First of the Crazies

Mister, I'm not like the other crazy people.

By Brent Curry

"First of the Crazies." That's what one Dawson City local called us as we scurried about town making final preparations for our epic bicycling trip. It seemed the old man had seen his share of young, daring bucks pass through Dawson's streets. Each summer the town's population swells with wild adventure seekers like the three of us, and I could tell from the resigned tone in his voice that he was less than thrilled this year's "crop of crazies" had turned up a few months ahead of schedule.

Whether we liked it or not, the old man was lumping us in with other questionable characters that we didn't even know. This hardly seemed fair. You'd think under the circumstances I'd have more important things to worry about than what some old man thinks, but such was my neurosis.

Plans for our expedition had begun when two friends of mine, Gary and Ray, had independently suggested eerily similar ideas. My two friends didn't know one another, yet they had each envisioned a trip involving the following rarely affiliated themes: bicycles, wintertime, and Tuktoyaktuk, Northwest Territories.

From the onset, I found the union of these diverse concepts terrifying and utterly unappealing. I'd thought to act as nothing more than an intermediary in bringing my two lunatic friends together so that they might discuss their lunatic ideas between themselves. Of course, I should have known they'd want me to tag along.

Ray had cycled the 725-kilometre Dempster Highway in the summertime and yearned to experience it in the winter. He also wanted to explore the ice road north of Inuvik that, during the winter months, follows the frozen Mackenzie River Delta all the way to Tuktoyaktuk. Gary was going to have a window of time free upon returning from a job in Australia, and coincidentally had a friend named Leila who was working in Tuktoyaktuk. Although Gary could have simply taken the bus up to see Leila, that's simply not the way this man rolls.

For my part, as much as I was frightened by what my two friends were scheming, I was also of the mind that if Gary and Ray were actually going to do this, I didn't want to be left out.

So there we were: Gary and Ray intent on riding a thousand kilometres of frostbitten Arctic road because it was there ... and me just wanting to tag along with my buddies. Never mind that the long-dead George Mallory was said to have applied similar reasoning for his desire to climb Mount Everest.

But motivations are different these days, and it seems that now, simple explanations like this no longer suffice. Whether folks are running a marathon or crossing the Kalahari on a pogo stick, it seems they've got to be raising money, or at the very least "awareness," for something.

So we asked ourselves, "What do we care about? What's near and dear to our hearts?"

Well, we all cared deeply about the planet. We all rode our bikes regularly, both for the sake of the environment and for the sheer joy of riding. It gave us some satisfaction to think that by doing something like riding our bikes to the Arctic Ocean, we might inspire people to use their own bikes more often, even if only to ride down to the corner store for some milk.

"Does that count?" we asked each other. We hoped so, because here's the thing: if you can convince people that what you're doing is not motivated by personal self-interest, but rather by some greater social cause, people will sometimes give you stuff. And as we had put together our list of required equipment for the trip, we had come to the realization that we were going to need quite a lot of stuff. With temperatures plunging to minus forty degrees Celsius (or worse with wind chill), everything from our footwear to our sleeping bags would have to be winterized and super-sized.

We would have to start planning a pretty ambitious marketing campaign for ourselves.

So we dubbed our trip "Roads to Resources," after the program of the same name initiated by Prime Minister John Diefenbaker. The Roads to Resources program was intended to develop transportation infrastructure into remote areas of Canada—for the purposes of oil, gas, and mineral exploration. The year of our trip was the twentieth anniversary of the completion of the program's first highway: the Dempster. Our plan was to commemorate the completion of the road with a bike trip, drawing attention to the natural beauty of the North and all its "non-commercial" resources. Or so we told our prospective sponsors.

While our mission statement might have sounded contrived and a little pretentious, the spirit was genuine.

Most gear suppliers no doubt saw right through our supposedly altruistic enterprise, but many offered to help us just the same. Sponsors gave us (or offered us) discounts on bike trailers, snow shovels, thermal underwear, dehydrated vegetarian meals, energy bars, sleeping pads, mitts, and gaiters to keep the snow out of our boots. The rest of our gear we gathered ourselves, a task that was still ongoing even in our final days in Dawson City.

Did we have everything we needed? We were never completely sure. The stakes were high on that front. That guy who had called us crazy had seemed friendly enough. But I couldn't help but detect a veiled insinuation that we latter-day Davy Crocketts had better not get ourselves lost or frozen out there, because if he had to come and rescue us there was going to be hell to pay.

On March 16, 1999, we rolled out of Dawson on studded tires, towing our trailers full of supplies. We didn't want to make a scene, but we did want to mark the occasion with some photographs and video footage. So we took our time rolling down Front Street and out onto the Klondike Highway, which runs for about forty kilometres before reaching the Dempster. It was a crisp clear day:

only about minus fifteen degrees Celsius. The three of us were ecstatic that all those months of preparation had finally come to fruition.

Just as we were relishing this feeling of self-satisfaction, Gary's chain shifted into the spokes of his rear wheel with an awful grinding noise and brought his bike to a screeching halt. His rear derailleur self-destructed like a taped recording from Mission Impossible. Our message, had we received it before it had mashed itself into Gary's rear cogs, likely would have been in Morse code. When translated, it would have gone a little something like this: "L-O-S-E-R-S-!"

We were only three kilometres from Dawson and already we had a mechanical issue that we were not equipped to deal with. Gary had a bent derailleur hanger on his frame and needed a new rear derailleur. With our tails between our legs, we headed back to Dawson. Needless to say, we took the back way into town.

With a renewed feeling of optimism, we headed out again the next day. The weather those first few days was about as nice as we could have hoped for. Our bikes were equipped with pogies— insulated coverings that snapped over the ends of our handlebars, enveloping our hands along with the bike grips, brake levers, and shifters. We found that right down to about minus fifteen degrees Celsius we didn't even need to wear gloves inside their quilted confines.

We were fortunate to have these, because for much of the first week we struggled with another mechanical issue that we repeatedly froze our hands trying to fix. The drive-side spokes on Gary's rear wheel had been gouged in the earlier derailleur debacle. One by one, they gave way. At first, it was clear what we needed to do: stop and replace the broken spokes so Gary's wheel wouldn't collapse under the immense weight of the loaded bike and trailer. We would replace one or two broken spokes at a time, then hope that the rest of the spokes would hold.

Eventually, however, things got tricky. We ran out of spokes.

For lack of any better ideas, we began twisting together pairs of broken spokes to create single functional ones. Gary's wheel wasn't going to be winning any beauty contests, but then again, that ship had pretty much sailed on this ancient hybrid bike of his anyway.

Our trip was timed around the vernal equinox (March 21st), so our days consisted of close to twelve hours of daylight and twelve hours of darkness. We would rise with the sun and start melting snow with our white-gas stove to make oatmeal porridge. As one person cooked, the other two packed up the tent. We generally didn't linger too long over breakfast, knowing we wouldn't be truly warm again until we were back on our bikes and moving.

Through the day, we stopped at regular intervals for snacks: mainly trail mix and energy bars. We pre-warmed the energy bars by placing them in the EZ Bake oven (and by EZ Bake oven, I mean down the front of our undershirts). We also drank continually from backpack-style water bladders, which we wore underneath our jackets to keep the precious liquid from freezing. We would keep up that routine until around 4:00 or 5:00, then stop to make camp. To conserve energy, we generally didn't venture too far off the highway to pitch our tent—maybe fifty metres at the most.

For dinner, we rotated through rice, couscous, and dehydrated potatoes, topped with soy-based dehydrated curries, tomato sauces, and chili. We stirred in an obscene amount of butter—one half-pound per meal, split between the three of us. Under any other circumstance, I'm sure I would never be able to stomach such buttery gruel. However, we were burning eight thousand calories per day just staying warm and hauling our heavy bikes down the highway, so we craved it. This "gruel" tasted like heaven.

Anytime we had the stove out, we melted snow for drinking water—about twelve litres every day. Each night, we had to take our water bladders into our sleeping bags so they wouldn't freeze. One night as I settled into my sleeping bag, I got a funny feeling that something wasn't quite right. I looked down and realized that one of the water pouches had not been sealed properly. Water was gushing all over the floor.

Acting fast, we tossed everything out of the tent, and thankfully it didn't turn into the crisis we had feared. At thirty degrees below zero, the water froze almost instantly, so we simply lifted the tent and shook the solid slab of ice from the floor. A few other items got wet, but we simply beat them with our hands until the ice crystals shattered and fell to the ground.

Our leaky water pouches were not the only things freezing inside the tent. Each night, condensation from our breath formed frost on the walls. In the morning it literally snowed on us as we rustled around changing into our daytime clothes.

One of the most bizarre effects of the extreme cold was manifested in the poles of our four-season dome tent. One night, as usual, we unfolded the tent pole sections, which are connected by an elastic shock cord, and began sliding the pieces together. Somehow, the shock cord had lost its elasticity and oozed out limply between any two sections of pole that one of us was not actively holding together.

The three of us scrambled back and forth along the four-metre length of pole, trying desperately to get all the pieces to stay put. It was like the world's most annoying game of Whack-A-Mole. No sooner would we get the shock cord tucked away between two pole sections than it would pop out again between two more at the other end. Finally, we gave up and sliced the cord with a knife, removing it altogether. From then on, we assembled the poles from the loose segments, trying not to lose any of them when we took the tent down.

At times, the cold was mind-numbing. Ray chipped a tooth trying to bite into a frozen Powerbar. The grease in our hub bearings refused to flow. The levers on our bike pumps snapped, and our facemasks grew rigid and became encrusted with ice.

Far worse than the cold, however, was the wind. It could be diabolical. When we reached the Eagle Plains Hotel and Service Station—roughly halfway between Dawson and Inuvik—the highway north of there was actually closed because of the wind.

The section of the Dempster that lay ahead was known as Hurricane Alley. When the winds blow strong, they can knock transport trucks right off the road.

That night, although we camped beside the hotel, we first enjoyed a bit of time inside the warm hotel bar. The bar was crowded with long-haul truckers and other stranded travelers. As usual, I wondered what some of these brawny truckers thought of us three weenies on bicycles, but for the most part it seemed we had earned their respect, having ridden as far as we had. Most had already seen us biking, and some had even stopped to chat when they had passed us further south, so this was a reunion of sorts.

The next day we heard the highway would be reopening, so we rode our bikes around the barricade, anxious to get a head start on the truck traffic that would soon be barrelling down the hill into Hurricane Alley. Eventually the procession of trucks caught us and we exchanged honks and waves as the truckers passed. A van full of German tourists passed us, too. Eight of them spilled out onto the road and jostled for the best camera angle, some of them lying on their bellies in the snow. I wondered momentarily if we should stop to talk, but as we drew nearer, it became apparent that these nature photographers were of the type who prefer to capture their subjects undisturbed, behaving as they would in their natural environments. So we pedalled past, frozen snot dangling from our noses.

That night, we ventured deeper into the bush to set up camp out of the wind. Gary wandered back toward the road and encountered one of our trucker friends struggling to reattach the tarp that had blown off the back of his rig. After Gary had helped him with the job, the trucker reached into the back of his cab and presented Gary with an entire "two-four"—a case of twenty-four cans—of 7-Up.

As much as Gary appreciated the gesture, he knew these cans would be frozen and bloated before we could do anything with them. He did, however, accept three cans, which he promptly brought back to share with Ray and me. It was an odd treat to enjoy in the middle of the frigid Yukon wilderness, but it fit right in with our "all calories are good calories" diet.

Knowing that there are only a finite number of memories one can retain through one's life, the memories I would most willingly surrender from this trip (or at least repress to the deeper reaches of my mind), would be the days we spent riding from the Northwest Territories border to Inuvik.

The Dempster crosses the border between the Yukon and the Northwest Territories at Wright Pass in the Richardson Mountains. The summit, shrouded in cloud, was oddly calm when we reached it—the infamous calm before the storm. But as we descended more than eight hundred and fifty metres toward the Peel River Crossing, the wind picked up and the temperature plummeted. We had to resort to walking at intervals just to keep the circulation going in our wind-chilled extremities. My nose got so badly scoured by the elements that a huge dark scab enveloped it, all but dashing my hopes of entering Inuvik's Most Eligible Bachelor contest.

North of Inuvik stretched the last leg of our journey. We had been using studded tires for the entire trip, and they had been helpful. But they would be absolutely essential on the ice road north of Inuvik, which is exactly what it sounds like: a road made of ice. Looking down upon it, you can trace the fissures through the otherwise crystal-clear ice and watch the Mackenzie River flowing six feet below.

The day we left Inuvik was cold, but calm. The only wind was coming from the south, which served to speed our travels along the frozen river towards Tuktoyaktuk. Although the temperature was in the minus thirties, I wore only a fleece jacket, reveling in what felt like a balmy day compared to what we had already been through.

In such favourable conditions, we hoped we could cover the distance to Tuk in only two days. Sadly, as the road turned eastward and onto the vast Arctic Ocean, we were faced with another brutal headwind. There was no way we would make it in two. We bundled up in our down jackets and pushed onward at a pace that might only be considered respectable for molasses at that time of year.

Our studded tires provided a good grip on the slick road surface. However, that's not to say all of us didn't have numerous spectacular wipeouts along that hundred-and-eighty-kilometre-long skating rink. Most of our crashes were caused by grooves in the ice that had been left behind by the road grader. If we accidentally steered into them, there was no way to steer ourselves out. Our bellies were all over that road like hockey mascots tripping over their plush boot covers.

After three days on the ice road—and a full two weeks after leaving Dawson City—we rejoiced to see the small community of Tuktoyaktuk looming on the horizon in all of its prefabricated glory. Soon we arrived at the school gymnasium to find Leila wrapping up another day at work. We parked our bikes behind her apartment and went inside for hot showers and a celebratory dinner. Words cannot describe how much I enjoyed those simple pleasures.

That night we talked Leila's ear off, telling her story after story about our long and bitterly cold journey. Around midnight we moved out onto her back porch, where we watched the northern lights dancing above.

I wondered about any future so-called "crazies" who might wander the Arctic landscape. Would they lie in their tents playing contrived games about 1980s music trivia and movies? Would they laugh at each other as they stumbled through the snow in their long johns, looking for a place to pee? Would they amuse each other with ridiculous stories from their childhood?

I certainly hoped so. I hoped that any future crazies would see their journeys through to a safe and happy conclusion, and that they would all have a warm place like Leila's to celebrate so they could start planning their next adventure.

Since returning from the Arctic, Brent Curry has continued to defy the conventions of bicycle travel. Other trips have included pedaling a wheeled couch through Maritime Canada (see the Summit Studios anthology Mugged by a Moose*) and towing a sixteen-foot canoe behind a tandem bicycle to the source of the Bow River in Alberta's Banff National Park. Visit him at* **www.bikeforest.com***.*

Holy Crap

How much excrement can a guy take?

By Brian Andersen

It was Friday the Thirteenth and I had to visit some of my Chicken Feed Friends in Washington State. Sometimes you sense that a day just isn't going to turn out right, and that's exactly the kind of feeling I had that day.

I hail from Abbotsford, which sits smack in the middle of Canada's Fraser Valley, just east of Vancouver and north of the U.S. border. The outfit I work for is called In Season Farms; they're producers and handlers of organic livestock feed. I deliver product to our clients, who include farmers and agricultural businesses on both sides of the border, and on that day I was scheduled to do a cross-border run.

The Abbotsford Air Show was running, so the requisite morning detour to avoid traffic put me behind the eight ball for Seattle's Friday afternoon rush hour. My twelve-hour trip was quickly turning into fourteen. I arrived at the border, waited in line, and finally got through around 10:30. From there I headed south—loaded with organic feed, sitting high in my seat, with the sun already blazing hot.

I got to Bellingham, turned the radio to Seattle's 95.7, and started rocking to a ZZ Top oldie. The deejay came on, announcing that it was already 30 degrees Celsius and that the sold out Mariners/Dodgers game would play havoc with the already nasty Friday afternoon traffic.

Then I hit the first weigh scales at Bow Hill. The whole process can be nerve-wracking even if there's no problem. I pulled off the freeway behind a long line of eighteen-wheelers like cattle heading for slaughter. Within minutes, it was my turn to *Proceed slowly at three miles per hour*. Just as my truck was clearing the scale, the sign above me displayed the word *STOP!* and then *Back up until the red light flashes*.

Shit. As I backed up, my stomach began rumbling with frustration, further aggravated by the Wal-Mart Metamucil knock-off I had taken the day before. I seem to get a little bunged up from sitting in the truck so long, so at times I call in the reinforcements.

The next words that appeared overhead instructed me to *Park and bring all paperwork inside*.

As I entered the weigh-scale building, a young scale cop named Dunbar approached the desk and asked, "Are you the driver of that In Season truck?"

I told him yes.

"That's going to be $169. You're 200 pounds overweight on your back axle."

I set my papers on the counter, pulled out my reading glasses, and reached for my Canadian Tire MasterCard.

"Just kidding," said Officer Dunbar. "I'll give you a warning this time."

I thanked him for being so kind, to which he responded, "Just thank your stars Officer Dungstein isn't the one dealing with you."

Thinking Dunbar wanted to kibitz a little—and always ready for some light humour myself—I said something like, "With a name like Dungstein, he could probably give a trucker a real shitty time of it."

Well, from far in a distant corner of the very dark weigh scale building (the darkness adds an element of power for these wannabe coppers), I heard a man's voice say, "Did you need assistance, Officer Dunbar?"

My buddy Dunbar giggled and quietly noted that we had awakened the devil himself.

From around the corner appeared Mr. Robocop. He had a crewcut and wore Terminator sunglasses, a starched uniform, shoes that reflected the entire front of his body, and a belt that contained too many items for me to remember—but I will try.

Starting from the right of his crotch there were four sets of keys, all color coded and hanging in order of length. Next to the keys dangled a heavy rubber sap, a five-D-cell-sized flashlight, and another sap, this one thin and telescopic. Next came a two-way radio, mace, handcuffs, leg irons, and leather gloves. These were followed by a pouch containing rubber gloves and KY jelly (gulp). Then came his cellphone, followed by a couple more sets of keys.

And last, but certainly not least, was a taser gun. He was clicking this on and off, causing sparks to bounce off the tile floor.

As he approached the desk, the sun hit his polished badge and caused my contacts to suck up against my already dry eyeballs. It was at that precise moment that Dunbar asked me to sign the overweight-warning document. Totally blind, I reached for the pen on the counter and knocked over Dunbar's coffee mug.

As the coffee made its way off the counter, it landed on Dungstein's shoes. Holy Mother of God. He did a hundred-and-eighty-degree airborne Karate move, whipped out his telescopic sap, and smashed it onto the counter.

I jumped back and farted.

Dunbar leaped up and positioned himself between me and this psycho—just as he was reaching for his taser and the KY pouch—and yelled out, "Stand down, soldier!" This sent Dungstein running back around the corner like a scolded child.

Dunbar stared at me with bulging eyes and told me to leave immediately. He did not have to tell me twice. Later, I would learn that this Dungstein character had just returned from a lengthy mental illness leave.

I jumped back into the truck, fired up a Camel Turkish Jade, and put the pedal to the metal. It was now noon and thirty-four degrees Celsius, and I had a vague feeling that I was in for a very long day indeed.

My first stop was on Highway 20, west of Burlington, at Skagit Valley Co-op. This was not really a Co-op, just an old hippy farm acting as a middleman for distributing In Season feed. As I turned into the horseshoe driveway at about 12:30 and positioned my truck to unload, I realized that moving the one-ton skids of feed would be no easy task. The driveway was on a slope and was cluttered with overhanging limbs from the many trees. The doorway to the shed was very low and narrow, and the cement floor was littered with old straw.

I cleaned the floor as well as I could with a pitchfork, pushed the first one-ton skid of bulk feed onto the hydraulic tailgate, and lowered it to the ground. As I turned the feed around, I misjudged the amount of slope towards the barn. Gravity kicked in, pulling the 2,000-pound pallet toward me until it pinned my back against the upper wall of the shed. The handle of the pallet jack jammed against my crotch, and the weight pressed my backside up against the wall above the doorway.

My feet were off the floor, so I had no way of getting any traction to push out and free myself. I was completely stuck.

For the next twenty minutes I hollered for assistance, but nobody was around. It was about this time that the dam of my inner sphincter gave way; it could no longer hold back my Wal-Mart stool softener. My only saving grace was that the wall above the door was pressing into me just below my butt cheeks, which mercifully stopped the "explosion," when it came, from dribbling down my legs. Instead, the pressure forced everything to rise toward the opening in my crewneck shirt, stopping somewhere in the vicinity of my third vertebrae.

What a mess I had gotten myself into! I pulled out my Leatherman tool, trying to remember if there was a saw that I could use to cut through the handle of the pallet jack—or my legs.

Just then, Ms. Spoonworth arrived home to feed her turkey chicks. I thanked the Lord that her automatic feeders had quit working the day before; if they hadn't, I would have been buzzard bait. The blowflies and wasps were already swarming around me.

Ms. Spoonworth gasped in horror as she came around the back of the truck. I told her not to be alarmed, and explained that she needed to hop in the truck and drive FORWARD. SLOWLY.

Unfortunately, we soon discovered that my keys were in my pocket, wedged up against the upper part of the pallet jack.

Ms. Spoonworth ran into the house and returned with a pair of her daughter's school scissors, which she hoped could cut through my shorts and free the keys. She was shaking as she reached forward, and due to the region she would be cutting in, I have to admit I felt a bit nervous.

With some relief, I soon realized the paper scissors were not going to work. My relief lasted until I heard her next idea: a pair of very dull pruning sheers.

She convinced me that she should try ... and did, carefully ... but it was a no-go.

Next, she grabbed a sledgehammer and suggested banging the handle until it bent back far enough to free me. I *begged* her not to do this.

We thought for a few moments. (Amazingly, she hadn't yet commented on smelling anything unusual). Eventually, it occurred to me that she could hook a chain to the front of the truck, then pull it forward slowly with her own truck.

This worked quite well at first, and I soon came free and fell to the ground. As she continued pulling, however, the forward motion of the vehicle began to tip the enormous bulk feed bag over—directly above me.

I screamed at Ms. Spoonworth to stop, but she didn't hear me, and soon I was buried under an avalanche of organic pig feed.

When she realized her error, Ms. Spoonworth slammed on the brakes and ran to the back of the truck. She jumped on the pile of feed and started digging through, working to free my nose and mouth. I came up gasping for air.

As I crawled out of the pile, Ms. Spoonworth made some comment about a rank smell. I was quick to blame it on the new soy product. "It may smell like crap, but the pigs love it in their feed," I lied.

I offered to shovel the feed back into the bulk bag, but Miss Spoonworth insisted she would take care of it. I thanked her and walked backward to the truck, so as not to expose the mess on my back.

I threw an old raincoat onto the seat, fired up the truck and a Marlboro Extra Light, then disengaged the emergency brake and wheeled away, wondering where I could cleanse myself.

Soon I reached the outskirts of Mount Vernon. I found a desolate spot on the banks of a meandering river, where I stripped down and washed both my clothes and myself. I was still waist-deep in the water, wringing out my Air Jordan T-shirt, when I heard a voice booming through a bullhorn.

"Put your hands in the air, turn around, and walk slowly towards me!"

Great! It was a female voice, and I was buck-naked. I wondered whether turning around and walking out of the water with my hands up was such a good idea.

A second blast on the bullhorn reminded me I had few options.

So I took a deep breath and turned slowly toward Officer Maria Bonito-Sanchez. Fortunately, her reaction amounted to nothing more than a muffled giggle.

You can say what you want about state troopers, but I'm here to tell you they're not so bad. If you get caught with your pants down and tell the truth, you will soon find yourself sitting beneath the shade of a weeping willow tree, sharing a two-litre jug of iced tea and laughing about your misfortunes.

I looked at my watch and told Maria that as much as I was enjoying the moment, I had to get going. She handed me my dry shorts that had been draped over one of the willow limbs and we kind of did a shake/hug before we parted. As I pulled away, I heard her voice echo through the bullhorn: "Adios Amigo!"

I think it's safe to say that on this day, I had already put up with more crap than any man should have to deal with.

Brian Andersen is currently semi-retired. When he is not golfing or in his kitchen trying out a new recipe, he works for In Season Farms delivering organic livestock feed. He and his wife live in Chilliwack, BC, and are looking forward to announcing the birth of two new grandchildren.

A Porcupine Ate My Cabin

Lessons learned the hard way are still learned …
but they can sure cost a lot of money.

By Bruce Day

When you are young, your life experiences and world view are simple, like the outer layer of an onion. As you mature, you discover that the onion has many, many layers.

When I was twenty-one years old, I purchased a fifty-acre forested property near Markdale, Ontario. I was studying landscape architecture and horticulture because I had always enjoyed spending time outside, beneath Ontario's diverse forest canopy. Sugar maples and black cherries, white ash and yellow birch, basswoods and cedars; the list is endless. Hiking and camping were my weekend activities, pursuits my dad and friends had always encouraged and supported when I was younger.

My friends and I enjoyed things in a very simple way when I first started driving up there from Toronto, where I lived at the time. We slept in tents and used an elevated horizontal log for answering calls of nature.

We didn't realize we were not alone.

My first attempt at building something was an outhouse. (I had begun to yearn for improvements to the facilities to prevent bruised hips and slivers.) So I recruited some friends and family members and we built it out of three-quarter inch plywood, with creosote painted on the bottom four feet of the walls and door. We were very proud of that outhouse for the first few weeks. The new plywood, however, must have smelled to the resident porcupines like turkey and stuffing smells to us. They had soon eaten a hole through the side; next, they began eating away at the insides of the walls.

So we installed aluminum printing sheets around the bottom of the outhouse, roughly three feet high. With this protection installed, I felt sure that my challenges were over.

A few weekends later, I arrived to find that in addition to plywood glue, a porcupine's diet includes aluminum. They had chewed another hole straight through the aluminum and the plywood, and had structurally destroyed the outhouse. The building was teetering, and when I looked inside I began to understand why. The critters had eaten through eleven-sixteenths of the twelve-sixteenths of plywood on the inside walls, as high up as they could reach. They had also devoured the entire vertical splashboard under the front of the toilet seat, along with at least ninety-five percent of the horizontal sheet that the toilet seat sat upon.

In essence, the seat was hovering above a gaping emptiness. All that was keeping it up was the five percent of wood still intact around the hinges. I guess the porcupines had somehow known when to stop eating. I'll bet you could have put a dime on the toilet seat and watched the outhouse collapse. There was nothing to save, so I destroyed it and used what little material remained to fill a low area nearby.

I was beginning to realize I was not alone.

There was a half-acre clearing on my property, and my next project was figuring out what to do with it. After much thought, I decided to fill it with some beautiful red pines. I planted two hundred in the clearing, thinking I was doing the resident deer a favour. I figured they could use the trees for shelter from the winter winds.

The new trees, however, must have smelled to the porcupines like turkey and stuffing smells to us, because those poor trees never reached twenty feet in height. They were so badly chewed and girdled by the porcupines that I had to cut them down and use them to fill low areas nearby.

I now *knew* I was not alone, but I didn't learn.

Porcupines are nocturnal, which means it was rare to see them around the property. One day, however, one of them came unexpectedly to visit while I was entertaining some friends and family. *Here's my chance*, I thought. *It's time to teach this fellow a lesson, make sure he knows he's not welcome.*

I found a large wooden box, approached slowly, then quickly dropped the box upside down over the porcupine. I set fire to some paper and dry grass inside the box to "smoke him out." A few of us banged on the outside of the crate and made lots of noise, hoping that when we let him out he would waddle away as fast as his stubby legs could take him. I figured we would never see him again.

We could hear him sneezing inside the smoky crate, so I figured he'd had enough. I turned over the crate to release him, whereupon he waddled purposefully to the first tree, climbed straight up, and then spent the next several hours defecating all over our makeshift kitchen table. What a mess!

I knew we were not alone and I was *beginning* to learn.

My sixteen-year-old Volkswagen Beetle was becoming ornery, and one winter day that year I had to leave it at my property due to mechanical problems. I caught the bus home to Toronto, and by the time I was able to return, it was late spring and my Beetle had been sitting in the snow and cold all winter long.

My "friends" had discovered my only means of transportation, and I guess the road salt on the tires must have smelled to them like turkey and stuffing smells to us, because all four tires were so badly chewed that they looked to be the thickness of one-ply toilet paper. They also ate the tire from my wheelbarrow, and the taillight covers on my sad-looking car.

I was beginning to learn, but I was learning the *hard* way.

The project for that next year was to start on a cabin. But this time, construction was going to be different. My friends, family members and I were not going to use plywood, glue, aluminum, red pine, rubber, plastic, or any of those foreign products made by man. I decided to use materials right from the local forest so that the porcupines could live in harmony with their invaders. The porcupines were there first, I realized, and I figured that if we were sensitive to their home, we could all live in harmony.

We were building a ten-sided post-and-beam building. It would have ten posts on the outside perimeter, five posts in the middle of the building, and one post in the centre. I planned to have a ground floor, a second floor ten feet higher, and a loft twenty-five to thirty feet off the ground.

We worked hard that summer. We dug the holes for the maple posts and concrete footings by hand; sifted the excavated products to separate sand and stones, also by hand; and cut down maple trees with a two-man saw and peeled them. We stood the poles up in the holes with the use of a block and tackle. We hauled water by hand from a creek down the road and mixed thirty tons of concrete on sheets of plywood. It was a *huge* amount of work, but we didn't mind. We would soon get to enjoy the fruits of our labour.

When I returned the next spring, a funny thing had happened to the cabin. We had left it the fall before with two floors complete and the roof on … but the porcupines had found it. Those critters had chewed through the ten-foot poles like beavers and brought this large structure to its knees in short order. It had collapsed and slid into a shallow valley, another low area of the property.

I was distraught, but I was also *determined* to stay and enjoy this beautiful wooded property. Porcupines or not.

So my longsuffering friends and I built a small cabin with a sheet metal skirting around the bottom. I encouraged the guys to "mark their territory" on nearby trees. This strategy worked, and I haven't had problems for years.

I now get along just fine with the porcupines.

I have learned a lot about these animals that roam the woods at night, and I believe strongly that they have as much right to be here as we do. After all, they were here first. Humans are so different. We have money and expensive tools and we plan our work extensively before we start. Porcupines plan nothing and do everything with their teeth ... teeth that continue to grow if they don't grind them down.

The porcupine motto is pretty simple: if you want to stay alive, keep on chewing!

Bruce Day still owns "Heartwood" —his property near Markdale, Ontario—and spends as much time there as possible. He also enjoys hiking, canoeing and exploring the Bruce Peninsula and nearby Beaver Valley with friends and family.

Sarong Song

I'm cold and turning blue, and why is this funny
salamander thing tied around my neck anyway?

By Matt Jackson

Sputtering and spitting water from their mouths, my friends Kirk and Trevor washed up along the banks of the river and found a bright yellow sarong peeking from the shoreline vegetation. One of the waterway's largest rapids had flipped their canoe, and they had just finished conducting a "fish count" below Saunders Ledge. Glub. Glub.

Now Kirk was wearing the salamander-print sarong like a superhero's cape, dancing around like an inebriated chipmunk with hemorrhoids. He would later attach it to a makeshift flagpole at the stern of their canoe.

Kirk and Trevor were the first casualties of my bachelor party—a three-day canoe trip down a punchy section of Alberta's glacier-fed North Saskatchewan River. They would not be the last. As bachelor parties demand, there would be bravado. There would be antics. And with the river running high, there would be a lot of dumping, flipping, and getting wet—a lot of "fish counts." The sarong became the token passed from one canoe to the next as participants lost their "whitewater virginity."

There were ten of us on the trip, including myself, and it was the perfect chance to renew old friendships while others got to know each other for the first time. Participants spanned thirty years of my life, and it was the first time everyone had come together for a guys' trip. It was a memorable occasion.

That first evening we camped on a large sandy island about five kilometres downriver from Saunders Ledge. We pulled beer from the coolers, found a prime swimming hole, and cooked fajitas for dinner. We started a small fire, which became the center of the universe for one night of raucous storytelling, the tales morphing and changing and becoming more exaggerated by the hour.

Day two brought more rapids, including two large wave trains that were not marked on our map. It was at one of these unmarked rapids that Cam and Jason executed a perfect "half Eskimo roll" (flipping over, but not back up) and earned the salamander sarong for the first time. Glub. Glub. They swam ashore, dumped water out of their canoe, and changed into some dry clothes. Then, half a kilometre downriver, they performed the other half of the Eskimo roll. Glub. Glub.

Mid-afternoon brought us to one of the longest and most challenging rapids on the river: The Devil's Elbow. We pitched camp so we could practice counting fish and executing half Eskimo rolls for the remainder of the day. There are distinct advantages to not having female sensibilities along on such a trip, hounding you with useless observations like: "Your lips are turning blue and I can't feel your pulse. Maybe you should take a break for dinner rather than do another run." By the end of the day Brad and I had both tasted the drink for the first time; Trevor went in for a second time, while Cam completed his "hat trick." Glub. Glub. Glub.

If days one and two had their fair share of whitewater, day three was to be the grand finale. Of fourteen rapids worthy of note on our route, fully half of them were slated for day three, including Brierley's. At high water, Brierley's features a long and challenging wave train with huge standing waves, followed by a massive recirculating hole—unquestionably the crux of the entire trip. We were pumped.

We all managed to stay dry that morning, and apart from Mark and I almost running over a black bear that was swimming across the river, there were no major incidents. By early afternoon we had beached our canoes on a gravel bar to scout the churning water of Brierley's. The fact that we watched three teens successfully shoot the rapid in a large, pink inflatable pool made us feel only marginally better.

At this point, six out of ten in our group had tasted river water at least once. The pressure was on the remaining four to preserve their reputations. Jason and a second friend named Trevor went first. They made it through the Brierley's massive wave train, but were stopped dead on top of the huge hole. They clawed at the river frantically for several seconds ... then were sacked. Glub. Glub.

Next it was me and my friend Mark. We punched through the hole at the end, but had taken on so much water while bucking the wave train that our swamped canoe sank slowly below the surface a few seconds after shooting out the far end. Glub. Glub.

Only Wayne and Greg had their virginity intact, and all of us were pulling for them to lose it in spectacular fashion. They entered the wave train at a slight angle, but managed to recover before hitting the largest section. They pitched up and down wildly, maintaining a delicate equilibrium as they approached the large hole. Just before they hit it they let out a resounding *Whooop!* and plowed successfully through. Their canoe fluttered briefly, but stayed upright.

As they cruised past, I called out: "I love you guys, but I just want you to know that you're both bastards."

In the end, Wayne and Greg weren't able to hang on to their whitewater virginity after all. As they approached the boat launch in Rocky Mountain House, a funny thing happened: their canoe inexplicably flipped not three metres from shore. They claim it had something to do with the eight guys leaning heavily on one of their gunwales, but I don't buy that for one second. Glub. Glub.

Matt Jackson is the president of Summit Studios and author of the award-winning book The Canada Chronicles: A Four-year Hitchhiking Odyssey. *It's been nearly a year since his bachelor canoe trip and he still hasn't dried off.*

The Patron Saint of Unconventional Car Repairs

Now if only he wouldn't talk quite so much.

By Kate Inman

When I was twenty-five years old, I drove from Hamilton, Ontario to Vancouver, BC in three days. It's around fifty hours by car.

The year was 1990 and I was driving an old Ford Escort I had bought from a friend of a friend just a few months earlier. It was my first car and I was the epitome of a young and naïve car owner. Before we made the transaction, the seller had asked if I wanted to look at the engine. I'd looked at it because it seemed like what one should do when buying a car, but the only thing I had truly been able to surmise was that, yes, the car *did* in fact have an engine.

I had been considering a move to western Canada for months. I wanted to be in the mountains and was seeking employment at an outdoor centre on Vancouver Island. When the call came that I was to be employed for their upcoming season, what had merely been a consideration needed to quickly become a reality. My start date was less than two weeks away.

I was young and naïve, but I was also resourceful. I wanted to keep my car, so the obvious thing to do was to drive to BC. I also wanted to spend as little money as possible and travel quickly, not wasting time and money stopping at motels. I decided to find some passengers who would be able to help with the driving and the gas expenses. So I put an ad—short and succinct—in our local paper.

Looking for passengers to share costs driving to Vancouver in my car. Leaving A.S.A.P. Call Kate. XXX-XXXX.

My friends thought I was crazy. My brother laughed. I won't even start on how my mom felt about the whole thing. At least she knew better than to try talking me out of the plan.

Within a couple of days of the ad being published, I had two passengers ready to go. One was Debbie, who was returning to Vancouver Island after visiting with her family; the other was Roger, who was going to visit his sister in Calgary.

Little did I know the important role Roger would play.

Roger was a forty-something man with a weathered leather jacket and worn canvas duffle bag. We met with a friendly handshake on the morning of our departure. Roger was also a storyteller, and he drove me and Debbie nuts with his constant chatter. His stories started before we left Hamilton, and they continued incessantly. Debbie and I quickly formed a secret alliance, agreeing that being around Roger for too long could possibly drive us to insanity.

Nevertheless, with his amazing resourcefulness and optimism in desperate moments, he would soon become my savior. I fondly think of him as Roger, the Patron Saint of Unconventional Car Repairs.

That first evening, driving along the northern shores of Georgian Bay, Debbie and I began to regret having Roger along.

We'd driven up through Sudbury and were heading to Sault Ste. Marie. The sun had set long ago and the road was very dark—and it was Roger's turn to drive.

He jumped behind the driver's seat, pulled onto the highway, and kept talking. And looking at us. You see, Roger was one of those drivers who need to look at their passengers when telling a story.

I remember thinking, *Oh dear, he's even using his hands for emphasis. I really want Roger to keep his eyes on the road and his hands on the wheel. Really.*

Miraculously, my wish came true. Roger started concentrating on his driving. He hadn't stopped talking; he was just changing subjects, now talking about the road.

"Man, this road is getting slick," he said. The car swerved gently and glided a few inches into the oncoming lane. I felt myself tense. I was not great with this sort of stuff.

"Real slick," Roger continued.

Suddenly a car coming toward us heaved into our lane, fishtailing out of control and forcing us onto the gravel shoulder at the edge of the highway.

"Holy shit!" I exclaimed.

The other car somehow corrected itself and continued in the other direction. We stopped at the side of the road.

Roger opened his door and put his foot down on the road, then slid it back and forth.

"Yup," he confirmed. "It's like a skating rink out here."

I took stock of the situation, which was looking increasingly dismal. It was March in northern Ontario; we were in the middle of nowhere; there were no lights to be seen anywhere; and beneath us was a road like an ice sheet. I was with two people I really didn't know, one of whom was quickly getting on my nerves.

While I tried to figure out our next move, Roger started driving again. He tentatively tested the brakes and discovered that my car would begin sliding sideways with each bit of pressure he applied.

"Roger, we can't keep driving on this road," Debbie said from the back seat. "We need to wait, at least until a salt truck comes by."

I silently agreed, although I wasn't sure how long we would last sitting in a cold car in frigid weather.

Roger disagreed. "We'll drive along slowly with one wheel on the gravel at the side of the road. That'll give us some traction."

We started moving slowly. Roger's plan seemed to be working, and after a few minutes my heart rate returned to a normal level. By this time it was past midnight, and we were all getting very tired. Incredibly, I started nodding off as we drove along.

Suddenly the car lurched and a crunching noise reverberated from the rear right corner of the car. Roger stopped and jumped out.

"We have a flat tire," he announced through the open door. "We probably ran over something on the gravel."

This was the point when our personal gong show truly began.

Roger was changing the flat before I'd even stepped out of the car. It had started to rain. The rain was very nearly snow, and stung like needles as it hit our faces and hands. Roger was lying on the ground, half under the car, setting up the jack. He was soaked. I wanted to help him, but was unsure of what to do. I huddled with Debbie and watched as Roger proceeded with the job.

Back on the road, Roger explained that the spare couldn't stay on indefinitely. "You'll have to get the other tired fixed," he said.

Reluctantly, I said I would buy a new tire the next day.

"No need," he replied. "We just have to plug the hole."

He'd found the reason for the flat; the tire had a nail right through it. Apparently, he thought he could fix it himself with a puncture kit.

I remember thinking, *Yeah, right.*

I humoured him by stopping at an all-night gas station outside the next town. He bought a kit for $3.99, then proceeded to wash, inflate, and plug the tire. After Roger replaced the spare with the newly fixed tire, we decided to drive into town and find an all-night restaurant where we could take a break and wait until first light, which was only a few hours away. Secretly, I doubted the repair job was going to last, and I wanted to give it a few hours before going back on the highway.

I laughed quietly to myself when we passed a sign with the town's name. It was called Marathon, and I surely felt like I was running one. It was four in the morning, so we began cruising the streets looking for a twenty-four-hour coffee shop.

That's when I became aware of another sound—a rattling, clanking sound coming from under the car. "Oh shit!" I said for the umpteenth time that day. "What now?"

Roger kept driving and I tried to ignore the noise until we pulled into the parking lot of a Tim Horton's. When I got out of the car, all I could see were Roger's feet. He was sprawled out on his back, hidden under the car again.

"Your muffler is loose," he announced as he shimmied his way out.

I groaned and muttered another expletive.

"I guess we'll have to wait until morning and find a place to get it fixed," I said.

Roger shook his head. "I think I can fix it."

There was a pause.

"But I'll need a coat hanger," he said.

I couldn't help it. I started laughing. For whatever reason, I suddenly found our situation hysterically funny. "A *coat hanger?*" I replied.

"And maybe a beer can," he continued.

Now Debbie was laughing, too.

As luck would have it, we managed to find what Roger needed to fix the muffler. The guy at the Tim Horton's steered us toward a motel down the road, and the night staff kindly donated a coat hanger. I'm really not sure to this day whether Roger did, in fact, use a beer can, but I like to think so. He was just that kind of guy.

Roger shinnied back under my car and did his thing. Debbie and I sipped our coffees, ate some donuts, and listened as the Tim Horton's guy told us the previous night's freezing rain had resulted in over a hundred and fifty accidents on the stretch of road we'd been travelling.

It was mid-morning by the time we were on our way again, cruising down the highway. Most people would be waking up and starting their days. I felt content and grateful in a numb sort of way. I was driving again, the muffler was silent, and the rear tire was holding up. Debbie was fast asleep in the back, and Roger was chatting away beside me. I still found his constant chatter annoying, but I felt so lucky to have him along that I dared not complain. Even to myself.

Later that day we crossed the Ontario border into Manitoba farm country. It was flat and we could see for what seemed like forever. It was around then that I noticed cold air blasting from the vents in the dash. I turned the knob to full heat. No change.

I turned to look at Roger. "You'd better pull over," he said. "Pop the hood."

Again, he jumped out of the car. This time I could almost see his superhero's cape billowing out behind him.

After a few minutes he came back with his verdict. "Your radiator has run dry. We need some antifreeze. We can't drive the car until we get some."

"Antifreeze?" I asked, my voice starting to crack.

"Coolant," answered a voice from the back. Debbie had woken up.

Roger was already scanning the horizon. I followed his gaze and saw a figure way out in one of the fields.

"I'm going to go ask that farmer if he has any antifreeze," Roger announced. He had walked across the ditch and into the field before I could answer.

This is a nightmare, I thought. I muttered more expletives under my breath. Debbie was silent.

We sat and waited. I wondered how I was going to get in touch with a tow truck. Finally Roger returned, and he was not alone. We heard him from a long way off telling one of his stories—one we'd already heard. We heard a female-sounding laugh.

"Hi guys," Roger shouted as he opened the car door. "Harriet says we can have some of her radiator fluid. She lives on a farm about a mile down the road." A woman stood beside Roger, wearing well-worn overalls and big farmer-style boots. She smiled at us.

We put the car in neutral and the four of us pushed the car to her farm. Harriet explained that she used radiator fluid for her pig-shit spreader. She disappeared into an outbuilding and returned a few minutes later with a one-gallon container.

Roger lifted the hood, took the container from Harriet, and began to fill the radiator. We all heard the liquid gush onto the gravel driveway beneath the car. Roger stopped pouring and put the container down, and once again he was on his back and under the car so fast I could hardly believe it.

"Looks like it's leaking," he said matter-of-factly.

He stood again and peered under the hood. Harriet leaned in, too. After a few minutes Roger re-emerged, announcing, "There's a split hose."

I moaned. *This is it*, I thought. *Our luck has ended.*

"Harriet, can I use your phone to call a tow truck?" I asked. Harriet nodded, but before she could speak, Roger interjected.

"Not to worry—we don't need to do that. I can fix it."

This time I just waited.

"All we need to do is replace the hose," he continued. "We can use one of the other hoses." His head ducked back under the hood.

"No!" I said firmly. I may not know much about cars, but I was sure that all of those hoses had a purpose.

Harriet agreed. "I don't think that's such a good idea, Roger," she said in her quiet manner. I wanted to kiss her. Roger backed down. He respected Harriet's word; they seemed to have bonded well in the last hour.

Roger was uncharacteristically quiet as he thought. "I know I can fix it," he muttered. He looked desperate, like he couldn't possibly let a simple radiator hose defeat him.

"I just need some hose," he said, almost to himself. "Any hose." I truly wanted him to succeed. I waited.

"All farms have hose lying around," he continued. His eyes scanned the farm, willing some hose to appear. "Harriet, don't you have an old hose lying around?" he asked. Harriet shrugged.

I am not exaggerating when I say that Roger looked heavenward at that very moment, and his eyes came to rest on a piece of hose. In a big old tree, not twenty feet from where the car was parked, an old piece of garden hose was hanging from a branch.

Roger was like a kid at Christmas. "There, in the tree!" he exclaimed. "Harriet, can we have a piece of that old garden hose?"

Harriet smiled. I don't think she would have been surprised if the hose had simply dropped out of the sky. "Of course," she replied. "Help yourself."

I'll never forget Harriet's farm. Debbie and I sat in her cozy kitchen having coffee while Roger, our Patron Saint, attached the old piece of hose with some clamps that Harriet had scrounged from a toolbox. She had a rusty-colored dog that nibbled part of my biscuit and sniffed at my crotch while I sat there. Harriet gave us a hearty wave when we finally rolled out of her driveway and set out across the Prairies again.

We didn't have another incident for the rest of the drive. By the time we said goodbye to Roger outside his sister's condo in Calgary, our mechanical problems were a distant memory. His stories had started to grate on our nerves again, and I can't say I was sad to see him go. But I must admit, I've often wondered how I would have fared on that trip without him.

Maybe my tire wouldn't have burst if we hadn't been driving on the gravel at the side of the road. Perhaps we would have been forced to get a motel, stop for the night, and give the old car the rest it needed. And maybe the muffler could have been fixed quickly and cheaply by a mechanic, and the radiator hose would have burst at a better moment. Like in a town, beside a garage. Maybe, maybe, maybe.

But then I wouldn't have this story to tell.

Since her memorable road trip from Ontario to BC in 1990, Kate Inman has settled nicely into coastal life. She currently lives with her family in Squamish and can be found either in the public library, where she does story times for children, or desperately trying to keep up with her son on the local mountain biking trails.

San Pedro Jail Break

An unexpected detour into Bolivia's most notorious prison.

By Jason Hoerle

It was probably the most fearful moment of my life. I was locked in a Bolivian jail cell with five convicted criminals, and nobody even knew I was there.

San Pedro Prison is in the city centre of La Paz, and it was the famed "gringo trail" that had led me there. My wife Lindsey and I were on a three-month journey of discovery from Quito, Ecuador to Santiago, Chile, and Bolivia presented us with a raw developing country blessed with glaciated mountains, lush jungles, unpopulated vistas, and affordable travel. The Lonely Planet guidebook offered advice about hostels, cafes, and adventures. One such recommendation was a "jail tour" of San Pedro. The book stated that tours of the prison were a highlight of La Paz, and that they offered some insight into the daily life of the world's most unique prison.

The "protocol" for gringos like us was to line up at the prison entrance daily, then wait for a prisoner to fetch an English-speaking "guide." The guards would let groups of travellers in and take a cut of the proceeds. Quite an organized business racket of sorts. Some gringos would even pay extra to stay overnight, then bribe guards and consume the purest cocaine in the world. Most of the inmates of San Pedro were there on drug-related offenses. Thus, the cocaine production and dealing did not cease behind the stone walls.

Lindsey and I had no interest in cocaine, but we did want to see the prison. We stood in line for two days, but to no avail. The Bolivian government had recently banned all tourists from entering. A posted sign from the governor stated that only wives and children could visit the inmates.

The jail tour was not to be on our "tick list" for La Paz after all.

The next day I ventured out for a walk while Lindsey retired for a midday rest. As usual, La Paz bustled with street vendors, food stalls, and the chaotic pace of urban life. I walked and took pictures, and to my surprise the route I chose brought me back to San Pedro. There were no gringos lined up, so I decided to approach one of the guards to practice my Spanish. To my surprise, a Bolivian prisoner motioned me over and offered me a tour of the prison. This was my opportunity!

We negotiated a price and an English-speaking guide was dispatched, a wiry German man named Hans, perhaps fifty years old, with a face that told a story. A great deal of commotion ensued that included a heated debate between Hans, the guards, and the tour coordinator. I felt uncomfortable being caught in the middle of the gun-toting guards, frantic wives in waiting, crying children, and Hans trying ever so hard to close the deal. But I realized another chance like this wouldn't come along, so I ignored my inhibitions.

At last I was shuffled past metal detectors and shoved into the prison grounds. Hans shook my hand and introduced me to four hardened and muscular Bolivian prisoners. "These men are for your protection," he assured me.

Fellow travellers we'd met had all informed us that the jail tour was a safe adventure. However, it was quickly sinking in that I had enlisted on a last-minute solo tour, and that my next of kin had no idea where I was.

The tour started with Hans's biography. He was a drug mule caught at the La Paz airport trying to smuggle cocaine back to Europe. He was condemned to a five-year sentence and was one of only ten English-speaking inmates out of more than two thousand. As we walked through the prison, two of the bodyguards walked in front of us while the other two trailed behind. The escorts gave me a sense of security, but Hans's glazed, red eyes did not put me at ease.

The prison was divided into sections according to a self-governed socio-economic system. No guards patrolled the interior of the prison. The prisoners voted for section leaders and formed their own democracy inside. Jail cells were purchased like real estate, including deed titles and sale agreements. The wealthier inmates could purchase larger cells that included private baths, televisions, and kitchenettes. The penthouse was owned by

Barbachoca, a drug baron caught trying to fly a plane carrying 440 tonnes of cocaine to Mexico. The $420 million cargo had been destined for the United States.

It was quite surreal to pass playing children, a football pitch, and small vendors serving all the prison staples. It's a prison, yet it seems to offer many freedoms to the incarcerated. The tour also covered the rougher sections where drug-addicted prisoners slept eight to a cell, and often spent days on drug-fueled benders. Hans told me that about four prisoners a month die from accidents and "natural" causes.

There's even a form of public justice at the prison, exercised at *la piscina*. The prison pool is filled with ice-cold water and the indicted person is submersed in the chill. Prisoners surround the pool brandishing sticks and rocks, then bash the victim until he's dead. Not surprisingly, parole boards, humane rights committees, and the media are not welcome at San Pedro.

Of course, corruption abounds in Bolivia, and San Pedro is no exception. The guards take a cut of the tour fees. Drugs and jail souvenirs are offered to the tourists. I was surprised to learn that Coca Cola has exclusive rights to peddle its soft drinks in San Pedro. They also sponsor a football tournament and provide team jerseys. If only the shareholders back home knew how the Bolivian "division" operates.

The tour was going well, but I never really felt comfortable. The euphoria of adventure was the only thing that kept me curious. My comfort level took a further nosedive when Hans suddenly became very serious, claiming he wanted to show me the voting room where prisoners were allowed to participate in municipal elections.

The four henchmen diverted us down a darkened corridor to a room that seemed more bomb shelter than electoral facility. The windowless walls were bare slabs of concrete. We walked in together and the iron door clanged loudly as it closed behind us.

The clang of the door was followed by the clicking sound of a latch falling into place.

As I turned around, I noticed that Hans held a key in his fingers and had a broad smile on his face. We were all locked in this cell and Hans, the lone key holder, appeared to find something amusing.

My dictionary defines fear as "anxiety caused by real or possible danger." My heart rate climbed and my anxiety became a series of flash-card images. I tried desperately not to imagine the reason a naïve tourist was now locked in a cell with five Bolivian criminals. I thought of Lindsey and my parents—no one knew where I was.

Hans began in a slow, dry tone: "Dis is de part of de tour where we all ..."

An icy chill ran up my spine. I felt dizzy, almost ready to fall over. Hans paused and asked me if I was all right.

"Fine," I responded. "You were saying?" I pictured a sidebar in a national newspaper somewhere in the world: *Canadian Tourist Missing in La Paz.*

How did I get here?

Hans started again: "Dis is de part of de tour where we all meet in secrecy, away from de odder prisoners."

"Fine," I replied. The four bodyguards moved towards Hans and me, forming a circle around us.

"It's really for de safety of you and me," Hans said. The four felons stared intently at the holder of the key as he spoke. "Vat happens now cannot be seen by de odder men."

I may have smiled back at Hans as a nervous reaction, but my mind was still racing and I could feel my palms growing clammy with sweat. Diabolical acts played out in my imagination. What was my exit strategy? Five jail-hardened thugs versus one white-bread, middle-class, pacifist backpacker—any bookie would guarantee those odds.

The room was silent. Five pairs of eyes watched for my next move.

"Now, I need to collect da payment," Hans continued.

Payment for the tour, I hoped.

I was carrying my money belt with limited Bolivianos hidden below my waist belt. To see the light of day and return to the hostel safely, I would have signed over my RRSPs and our home back in Canada.

"Forty Bolivianos, señor."

About five Canadian dollars was going to buy me freedom.

I unclipped my money belt and counted out the funds. The four Bolivians began to smile and the mood changed: the heavies would not have to beat me into paying after all.

To this day it remains the best five dollars I've ever spent.

As we walked back to the prison entrance, Hans explained that the room was the safest place in San Pedro to exchange funds, hidden from greedy guards and ruthless drug addicts.

In hindsight, it probably was not the most dangerous predicament I've found myself in. Protecting the tourists in San Pedro helps keep the corrupt systems in place. Those moments of fear were my perceptions of the scenario. It was an experience that keeps me reading faces and looking for that key to life.

Jason Hoerle lives in Canmore, Alberta with his wife Lindsey and their daughter Beatrice. The closest he gets to a jail cell these days is via a cleaning company he operates. They hold the contract to clean the Banff Court House and its holding cells, which is a pale comparison to San Pedro.

Bridge Over Troubled Water

For cryin' out loud … duck!

By David Lee

Some say that if you wish for something hard enough it will happen; others believe that wishing earnestly means it won't. I definitely belong to the first group, though I'm the first to admit the wishes granted to me don't always come up roses.

When I look back at various incidents in my life, there seems to be a frightening trend. You might call me overly curious, masochistic, or just plain stupid, but some of my wishes seem to involve experiencing things that most people prefer to avoid. For example, up until the age of fourteen I was lucky enough to have avoided breaking any bones, even though several of my friends had done so. I began to wonder what it would *feel* like to break a bone and be the center of attention. Not long after that, I was playing outside with some friends and decided to perform a gymnastic maneuver we had learned at school. It didn't occur to me that being bundled up in a thick coat and heavy boots (it was February) might hamper my ability to execute the flip. I landed in a cross-legged sitting position rather than on my feet and snapped my right tibia clean through.

For a time I also wondered what getting stung by a bee would feel like. I knew that the stinger gets left behind, that poison gets pumped into you, and that it hurts momentarily. But what does it *feel* like? Is it really all that bad? Not long after, one of the little bastards stung me on the face. Ouch! Ouch! Ouch!

Motor vehicle accidents involving large groups of people, such as buses and vans crashing, are a frequent topic of coverage in our mainstream media. Since I hadn't learned my lesson in the previous incidents, I began wondering what being in an accident was like. One day, while on a road trip with some friends, I got to find out. There must have been a dozen of us squeezed into a van, motoring along a country road at a hundred kilometres an hour. I was sitting directly behind the driver. At one point I remember looking out the front windshield and seeing an intersection at the bottom of a long hill. At the intersection was another van traveling perpendicular to us; it was stopped, but was exhibiting the all-too-uncomfortable lurch of can-I-make-it/no-I-can't syndrome.

The last thing I remember thinking was: "It better not!" But it did, of course—just as we were nearing the bottom of the hill.

The angle of the vehicle and the severity of the crash put me with the driver at the front of the impact. The force was so strong that it ripped the bench seats off the floor. I blacked out as my head smashed the windshield and bounced off the driver's side pillar, and I was later told that everyone and everything behind me had utilized my head as an airbag.

I love the outdoors. When I'm not breaking bones, getting stung, or smashing into windshields with my face, I spend as much time as possible outside, participating in activities such as hiking and biking. But the one activity I have a long-time love affair with is canoeing. Not just a Sunday afternoon paddle around the cottage, you understand, but big-time canoe tripping. The longer the trip, the better. The further away from civilization, the better. The rougher the conditions, the more thrilled I am. My brother has referred to me as a "canoe junkie," and it's quite possible that I *am* addicted!

In late April 2005, I had already developed the springtime itch. I wanted to get an early start on the paddling season, so I talked my girlfriend Marylou into joining me for an easy two-day float down the York River, not far from Bancroft, Ontario. The lakes were still iced over, but I was certain the rivers would be flowing. Of course, at that time of year it can still be quite cold in Ontario, so you want to avoid going into the water. But I wasn't concerned. There wasn't any whitewater on the river, just a few small chutes that we could easily portage around.

Or so we thought.

In any case, the technical nature of the trip was not a concern and I had never experienced a serious capsize before—though true to form, I had been curious for some time what capsizing and losing all your gear would *feel* like.

My brother and his girlfriend were supposed to join us, but they backed out at the last minute. They did, however, graciously offer to shuttle us to the starting point so that we could leave our own vehicle at the place where we would be finishing the trip. As we drove between these two points, we crossed a metal bridge that spanned the York. We noticed that the water level was very high—so high, in fact, that it was flowing less than a metre from the bottom of the bridge.

"I dare you to run your canoe under that," said my brother's girlfriend Kerry, giving me a wink.

Everyone but me shrugged off her ridiculous comment. I began plotting.

Some hydro workers at the put-in location informed us that the ice had gone out the previous day. I couldn't believe our luck: what timing! Shortly after pushing off, we discovered that the riverbanks were flooded and the current was indeed quite powerful. The temperature was also quite cold, and as we reached some of the chutes we had been expecting, we found not only raging waterfalls but also portages that were choked with snow. Regardless, we were in the canoe and I was loving every minute of it!

We ended the day at around the halfway point, just before some voluminous rapids that we hadn't been expecting. Based on information I had gleaned for the York, there had been no mention of rapids, but that was probably true for those who paddled the river during the summer. It was clouding over and beginning to rain, so we decided to stop, make camp, and then decide whether to run the rapids in the morning.

The next morning the sun was shining, and it looked as though we were going to have a wonderful day. I scouted the rapids and found that the water levels had dropped a bit, which meant the size of the waves had decreased. But they were still large enough to make our canoe capsize if we were not vigilant.

After some discussion, we decided that we would try to run the rapids, even though we were nervous because the waves were still big and the current very pushy. As we approached the whitewater, we carefully picked our line through the middle to avoid a large sweeper—a tree leaning out low over the river. The thrilling ride lasted only a few seconds, but we ran it like experts and shot out the far end with huge grins plastered across our faces.

Five minutes of paddling brought us to the metal bridge we had crossed in my brother's car the day before. I had been thinking about Kerry's dare—the quip she had made about paddling our canoe under the bridge—and I told Marylou that I wanted to take a closer look to see if it might be feasible. We walked up to the bridge and saw that the water was still running very close to the base of the bridge: there was perhaps a little more than half a metre separating the two. It occurred to me that if we crouched down inside the canoe, there would be more than enough room to pass underneath. We even did a test crouch, which confirmed that there would indeed be ample room.

Marylou was a little nervous about the whole idea, but I was not to be deterred. I pointed out that there were no rapids beyond the far side of the bridge, just a slothfully moving river. We talked through my strategy, then checked and rechecked the measurements, and after that she seemed more confident. She agreed to try it.

We paddled upriver to the staging point and finalized the procedure we would follow as we approached the bridge. I pulled out my new digital camera and set it to video mode so we could record our accomplishment to showcase later for our friends back home. With Marylou taking the bow position and me in the stern of the canoe, we began floating toward the bridge.

Here's the play-by-play account of what happened, noting the distance from the bridge in metres as we approached it:

10m: Marylou and I stopped paddling, allowing the canoe to drift with the swift current.

9m: Marylou put her paddle inside the canoe.

8m: I removed my camera from its protective Pelican case.

7m: I made a corrective paddle stroke to straighten the canoe.

6m: I turned the camera on and checked to make sure it was in video mode.

5m: I made another corrective stroke.

4m: Marylou started to crouch down.

3m: I vocalized our readiness.

2m: I made one more corrective stroke and pulled my paddle out of the water.

1m: I slid my paddle inside the canoe and started to crouch down.

At that instant, Marylou's head popped up. As we passed under the first beam she reached up and grabbed the underside of the bridge, stopping the canoe dead. I was perhaps as shocked as she was, but all I could manage in my bewilderment was, "LET GO!"

(We later determined that Marylou had a panic attack—the yawning dark maw of the bridge triggered something primal, and she reacted instinctively.)

Despite my vocal protestations, she was not about to let go. In a matter of seconds, the current grabbed the stern end of our canoe and swung it like a pendulum until it was broadside to the bridge. I had no choice but to join Marylou, and soon found myself sitting upright in the canoe with the video camera in one hand, my other hand holding onto the bridge for dear life.

Anyone who has paddled moving water knows that having a canoe broadside to a strong current can be a precarious situation, especially when you are pinned. As we sat there gripping the bridge and trying to maintain a delicate equilibrium, the canoe began tilting upstream under the force of the current. A few seconds later, the upstream edge dipped below the surface and water began pouring over the gunwale and into the canoe. It wasn't long before the weight of the water flipped the canoe over and whisked it, along with all our gear, under the bridge and out of sight.

And where were we, you ask? Hanging from the bridge like a pair of incompetent Navy Seals! I clung to the bridge with one hand, still holding the camera in the other, and managed to throw my right leg over a horizontal beam to keep me out of the water. Marylou's situation was worse; she held onto the base of the bridge with both hands while her lower half was submerged in the icy cold river.

I yelled at Marylou, encouraging her to climb up and over the bridge railing, but the power of the current and the weight of her wet clothes made this impossible. As I was in no position to help, I told her there was no alternative but to let go, pass under the bridge, and swim for shore. Eventually she couldn't hold on any longer; the river plucked her from the bridge and whisked her into the darkness.

I jammed the camera onto a small ledge, and with both hands free, was able to climb up a column and jump over the railing onto the surface of the bridge. Concerned for Marylou, I ran across the bridge and started searching the shoreline. Thankfully, she was fine. Her whitewater training had helped her compose herself; she had floated down the river with her feet out until she found a place to safely haul herself up on shore.

She was physically unharmed, but the chilly spring temperatures meant that hypothermia was still a danger. Far down the river, I could see our canoe floating upside down with the current. The only chance we would have to retrieve our gear— along with our camp stove and matches to light a fire—was if the canoe got snagged along the shore. Unfortunately, there was no way of knowing how far down the river that might be.

As we searched the riverbanks, we spotted a few cottages hidden among the trees. But before we could approach any of them, a vehicle crossed the bridge. The driver was a man named Harris Whyte, and after we explained our predicament he generously offered to help us find the canoe.

The first thing Harris did was drive us to his home so Marylou could change out of her wet clothes. We met his wife Eileen, who loaned Marylou some dry clothes and put her wet garments in the dryer. We then borrowed Harris's friend's canoe so he and I could paddle downstream to retrieve our own. We searched every metre of shoreline for more than a kilometre, but there was no sign of our canoe or any of our gear. Everything appeared to be lost, including the car keys.

Harris then suggested that we drive his truck to a place further downstream where the river opened into a marshy area. He explained that there was an outfitter located nearby on the bank of the river, and he was confident that with an absence of current in the marsh our belongings would stop there.

As we pulled into the outfitter's compound, we noticed one of our canoe barrels and one of our backpacks sitting on his deck. We later learned that the owner, his son, and some friends had been sitting on the riverbank enjoying a beer when they saw a paddle float by. One of them walked down and grabbed it. Shortly after that a pack floated by, and then a canoe barrel, and then finally the upside-down canoe with no paddlers in it. They wisely deduced that something had gone awry and called the local police and river-rescue team. They had reckoned they would be pulling bodies out, and we had arrived just in time to call off the search party.

This experience taught us some invaluable lessons, and perhaps more importantly, has reminded me once again to be careful what you wish for.

I wonder what it feels like to get hit by lightning?

Marylou and David still paddle together, even under bridges. David teased her about the bridge debacle for several months, until Marylou's finely perfected "death gaze" convinced him to stop. He prefers sleeping inside the tent.

A Winter's Tale

Outdoor experience can be highly overrated.

By Philip Torrens

I can still remember the year my best friend Jimmy arrived home in late March, fresh from his first semester at a chic private boarding school in Maine. Based on having survived a single night in a tent that winter—coddled by teachers, hired guides, and for all I knew, butlers—he had begun to reckon himself a cross between Nanook of the North and Daniel Boone.

It was therefore *his* suggestion that during my spring break—from my decidedly more down-market public high school—we should embark on an overnight hike directly from the suburbs of our small town on Prince Edward Island. When I expressed reservations, he assured me, "It'll be an adventure you'll never forget."

How right he was.

"Besides," he continued, "It's spring now. Winter is over."

We equipped ourselves with the best gear available. That is, the best gear available to a pair of kids hailing from a backwater town on Canada's East Coast. My rucksack was made by the Torquemada Rack & Pack Company and it had no hip belt. But that hardly mattered, since it had no frame, either. It sagged down my back like a sack of potatoes, forcing me to lean perpetually forward like a mime slogging into a non-existent wind. All our other gear was equally well designed.

The trip started well. The weather was sunny and mild, with the occasional patch of snow still clinging to life in the shadier groves. Official hiking trails being non-existent in our neighborhood, we followed a disused railway line out into the country. Our neck of the woods was more a neck of the fields, really. There are no old-growth trees on P.E.I.—indeed, there are very few trees at all—but a few of the farms do feature second-growth woodlots. One of these would have to do as our forest primeval.

Neither of us owned proper hiking shoes either, so we had to make do with our snowmobile boots. Frankenstein himself may have found these unwieldy blocks of rubber to be familiar footwear, but it was not so for us. We lurched along for several hours in mostly pained silence.

We eventually found a pretty little location in one of the bigger tree lots; the site even had a nearby stream. As we unpacked our tent, the following exchange took place:

"So, Jim, where are the tent pegs?"

"What do you mean? I distinctly remember *you* were going to bring the pegs…"

The tent itself was my dad's, a three-man department-store special: a nylon bungalow with a slippery floor made of polyethylene, replete with huge flat surfaces tailor-made to catch the wind like sails. A pair of spindly poles were designed to hold up our home away from home, one positioned at each end.

In what we considered a master stroke of woodsy self-sufficiency, we whittled replacement tent pegs from fallen branches (nearly whittling our icy fingers off in the process). Unfortunately, when we attempted to hammer our pegs in with the back of our hatchet, the pegs fractured against the icy ground, which had frozen as the temperature dropped in the late afternoon.

Casting about for alternatives, we kicked large stones out from the stream (at least our rubber boots were good for something). At first the tent's peg loops and guy lines slipped out from under these improvised anchors, but we soon discovered that if we stood on the wet rocks for a few minutes they froze to the ground, gluing the tent ties beneath them. The erected tent sagged like an ailing hot-air balloon, but it was the best we could come up with short of admitting defeat and going home.

By this time I was seriously chilled and feeling increasingly hungry. But I was determined not to cry; I whined instead. "Cheer up, Philip," Jim responded, "We'll have a roaring fire and a hot supper in fifteen minutes!"

An hour and half later we huddled over a small, smoky flame, trying desperately to coax it to life. In preparation, I broke out my one-person camp cooking set, which consisted of a frying pan with a handle that pivots to clip the matching plate in place as a lid for travel, with a little pot nested inside. In theory, such "mess kits" are a godsend; in practice, they're godawful. The foil-thin pan conducts heat with great effectiveness, allowing you to perform the reverse miracle of burning food on the bottom without getting it even lukewarm on the top. The bare metal handle conducts heat very well, too. If you forget this (and you inevitably do), your bare palm gets branded by way of reminder. And if the wing nut holding the handle (the hardware, not the cook) isn't tight enough, the pan inevitably rotates around it, decanting one's dinner into the flames.

The pot is likewise booby-trapped. The presence of a bail wire—or described more accurately, a tripwire—suggests that you can hang the pot cowboy-style over a fire. But in order to make it fit between the pan and the plate, the pot's designers made it much wider than it is tall, so it hangs in perfect counterbalance only as long as you don't try to do anything rash … like cook your dinner in it. Should you be so foolhardy as to actually add water, soup, stew, or any other liquid, the pot's hair-trigger equilibrium is instantly upset. As cookware goes, it makes an excellent fire extinguisher.

The aluminum plate is the mirror image of the pan. Appropriately, it performs the reverse functions: it sucks heat rapidly from any contents, simultaneously searing your hands and freezing your food.

Despite many fiascoes and singed fingers, we eventually finished cooking dinner. Hungry as I was, the charred, chilled beans I was shovelling into my maw actually tasted reasonably good. Then, for reasons unknown to this day, I set my nearly full plate down for a second, only to watch with dismay as it tobogganed down the icy creek bank and into the water.

The plate floated just long enough for the current to whip it out beyond the depth of our boots, shipwrecking itself a few seconds later against a mid-stream rock and sinking without a trace.

After my unexpectedly light supper, it was time to make ready for bed. In Jim's mind, essential preparations included dangling the pack with our remaining food over a high branch and tying the rope off as far up the tree's trunk as he could climb. This was to protect our larder from marauding bears. There hadn't been bears on Prince Edward Island for a hundred years, but that's what he'd been taught on his outing in Maine, so that's what we did. If his training trip had been in the desert, he would no doubt have insisted we check our winter boots for scorpions in the morning.

I inflated my rubberized canvas air mattress, which I would find that night had the insulating capacity of a stack of bricks. My sleeping bag wasn't any better; in my backpack it seemed roughly the size of a small sofa, yet it somehow provided less insulation than a burlap sack. We shivered uncontrollably for quite some time before exhaustion finally claimed us and we fell asleep.

I awoke several hours later from a strange dream: I had been lying in the middle of a field trying to fight my way out from under a windblown parachute. Oddly, even after I regained consciousness, I could still feel the flailing fabric buffeting my head. It took me a moment to realize a storm had blown up and the wind had unkindly snatched the pole lines from under their rocks and collapsed the tent on us. Outside, a thick, sleety snow was coating our world in white.

Jim and I quickly realized there was no hope of re-anchoring the pole lines. We deliberated through chattering teeth and decided to bring the poles inside, each of us curling around one of them to hold it upright. It wasn't particularly restful trying to maintain a tight fetal position around a rod that was being whipped back and forth by the wind, but it was better than having no tent at all.

After an age, my pole ceased its gyrations. In my half-sleep I figured this was because the wind had finally slackened. Not so. Upon inspection, I discovered it was because the part of the pole above my body had bent to a right angle and no longer held up any fabric to defy the still-furious wind.

At the first hint of daylight, we got up. Or rather, we gave up trying to sleep. Lacking mittens—we *were* on a springtime trip, after all—we slipped spare socks over our hands to protect our fingers from frostbite.

The trunk of our bear-cache tree was now sheathed in ice, as was the rope that held the pack. Of course, with socks over his hands, Jim's attempts to scrabble up the tree were turned back prematurely; indeed, he resembled a drunk lumberjack trying to shimmy up a greased pole with boxing gloves on. Next, he tried leaping as high as he could, but his limited "hang times" prevented him from undoing the knot.

After some minutes of this capering about, Jim decided to simply cut the rope with our hatchet. He backed up to get a running start, then charged with a mad gleam in his eye and a guttural "AAAAARRRRRRRRH!" that would have made a Viking warrior soil his animal-skin undergarments.

I can't remember whether it was on the ninth charge or the tenth that Jim's repeated axe swings finally severed the rope. But my memory lapse may have something to do with the lingering concussion I received when the released pack dropped directly onto my head. I collapsed in a heap beneath the backpack-turned-ice-bomb.

When I recovered, we extracted our breakfast oranges (I can only assume Jim included them to ward off scurvy on our overnight epic). They had, not surprisingly, turned into ice baseballs. These frozen treats unaccountably failed to refresh the way they would have done in, say, July.

Though the rocks anchoring the pole lines had let go, the ones holding the tent corners down were welded solidly to the ground by frozen sleet. We kicked at them half-heartedly, but not even our Frankenboots would dislodge them without breaking toes. Since it was my dad's tent, I knew I had to come home with it or I shouldn't bother coming home at all. It had cost a full thirty dollars, you know.

We pressed the hatchet head into service as a sort of prying wedge and eventually freed the tent, though it ended up with a couple of its corners amputated. Still, if I rolled it up tightly, stuck it in a far corner of the basement, and denied everything when my dad finally got it out for his spring fishing trips, I thought I stood a reasonable chance of escaping with my life.

Unfortunately, there was no chance the ice-crusted tent would fit back into its stuff sack. We eventually rolled it up as best we could, slung it over our shoulders, and beat our retreat home.

Linked by the awkward burden, we staggered and slid about in the snow like a pair of Arabic rug vendors who'd taken a seriously wrong turn somewhere on the Siberian Steppes.

Jim was right about one thing: it was a trip I'll never forget.

Despite this shaky start to cold-weather camping, Philip Torrens has since participated in multi-day ski tours and several winter and Arctic kayaking trips. The very worst that has happened to him (so far) was being gnawed on by a polar bear. Look for that story in Mugged by a Moose, *another Summit Studios anthology.*

These Sorels Are Made for Walking

The depths of cultural ignorance can be quite shallow.

By Karen Lewis

About ten years ago, my husband, our children and I moved to New Zealand in pursuit of work and adventure. We found a whole lot of adventure and a little bit of work.

We lived in a small city on the North Island called Rotorua—or "Rottenrua," as it is affectionately known. When we arrived, we stayed at the Pui Nui Motel (pronounced poohy noohy) across from the Whakawherewera Reserve with its famous spouting geyser. The sulfur smell was overwhelming; it occurred to us more than once that "Poohy Noohy" and "Rottenrua" were appropriately named. The only endearing thing about the motel was that it had its own private hot pool outside our room, which was a great benefit for jet lag after an eighteen-hour flight with two preschoolers.

About one year into our Kiwi experience, I got bored with my "corporate" housewife role and decided to apply for a job outside the home. My oldest daughter had started attending a bilingual Maori/English primary school where she learned about riptides and surfing and how to run cross-country without shoes. Meanwhile, my youngest offspring was enrolled in Free Kindergarten, where he learned how to dance the Haka war dance with pompoms and generally run wild like a Pacific Islander.

It was relatively easy to get a job in New Zealand back then. Even without a work permit, I was able to use my passport and apply for an IRS number. It helped that I had already applied for Landed Immigrant status and that my neighbor worked for the IRS. I got my first job there through a doctor friend: I became the coordinator of a continuing medical education program for the Bay of Plenty region. Then, after the junket money ran out, I looked for a more permanent position. One came in the guise of an employment advisor position with the New Zealand Employment Service. This is the Kiwi version of what's now known as Human Resources and Social Development in Canada, but with a twist. The "dole" (Welfare) and Employment Insurance divisions were rolled into one, so I worked with both short-term and long-term job seekers.

When I showed up for my job interview, I was asked if I had brought my supporter or *fanau* with me—a member of my family could speak on my behalf and act as my living, breathing reference. I hadn't known about the *fanau* thing, but it did make a whole lot of sense, as having my family there would have saved the interviewers a whole lot of effort trying to contact my references back in Canada.

I got the job and set to work in my little cubicle, proudly wearing my corporate uniform and carrying my corporate umbrella and corporate handbook to work. Work, Kiwi style, is hardly that. It is all about rugby, netball, after-work booze-ups, rugby, mystery tours, pub crawls, more rugby, and the occasional bungee jump thrown in for good measure.

My office was staffed mostly with Maori workers, who were the kindest, most giving and congenial people I have ever worked with. They were not above a good joke, however, and would often "borrow" the staff car, take it for a spin, and bring it back caked with mud and sporting an empty petrol tank. Then the offending party would swear on a deceased relative's grave that the car had *never* left the car park.

"Borrowing" seemed to be a major theme at the office, as I well found out at mealtime. I started to pack less appetizing lunches because if my lunch looked even remotely tasty, it would mysteriously disappear from the fridge.

There were also more comings and goings than you'd see on a soap opera. We never seemed to be fully staffed, as there was always a group away for a funeral or other ceremony of some sort. The office drama was very entertaining.

One of the most interesting subcultures I had contact with in New Zealand was that of the gang members associated with the infamous Mongrel Mob. They often referred to me as the "token *Pakeha*" (white person) and asked me if we had Maoris in Canada. This group came into my vision about the time the book *Once Were Warriors* surfaced in both New Zealand and Hollywood. The famous Ford Block was the postal code for many of my clients. These gang members, as long-term unemployed clients, would be required to check in with me on a regular basis. I loved listening to their stories. They were generally courteous and quite curious about me, as I was about them.

They showed up in customary leathers, imitating the North American gangs they had seen on TV. But it was their tattoos that fascinated me the most. They were elaborate and beautiful, usually traditional and tribal, reflecting their Maori heritage. For the most part the tattoos were professional, but some were garish and obviously done by amateurs. My favourite tattoo featured the letters BOM on the back of a gang member's bald head. I asked what BOM stood for and was told that it was a mistake; the young gang member had used a mirror and tried to tattoo MOB on the back of his own head.

As scary as they sometimes appeared, the Maori gang members had strange rituals that often seemed to me more funny than fearsome. For example, for all their tattoos and manly garb, they often wore white farmer's gumboots. I thought this made them look rather silly, especially in their big bad world of subculture. It wasn't until I learned that these were prized gumboots from the abattoirs, and that they were a status symbol granted to initiated gang members only, that I understood their significance.

All this cultural diversity fascinated me—so much so that my boss decided to take our entire office on a cultural road trip to the farthest reaches of the North Island, where we would meet the people we served. We started early one morning, filing into a rented school bus for our journey into the wilds of Urewera National Park. By the time we arrived at the *marae* (a sacred Maori meeting place, where we would spend two nights), I began to realize just how far we had come and how isolated we were. We had arrived high on top of a mountain range where the wind was howling and not a single city light could be seen.

We were warmly welcomed onto the *marae*. Taking a seat outside the carved red gate, we listened for our cue to proceed as the haunting ceremony to call on Maori ancestors began. It was all very moving and spiritual, but also incredibly cold. It was the middle of the southern winter. (I know that when most people think of New Zealand's North Island they think of the tropics, but it can also get very wintry.)

Fortunately, I had come prepared with my pink, slightly out-of-fashion Sun Ice ski jacket and my white Canadian "Snow Lion" Sorel boots, which insulate up to minus thirty-five degrees Celsius. I was smugly warm as I waited for our invitation into the *marae*.

I was dismayed, however, when I realized that I would have to take off my comfy Sorels when I entered the *marae* hall. It is customary to remove your footwear when you enter, as a sign of respect. No matter, I thought; I would still have my liners from inside my boots, which would be adequate insulation against the frigid, wooden floor. No sooner had I started to slip out of my Sorels than I heard an almost inaudible inhalation of breath from behind me. I quickly ascertained that I was being watched.

"Wher'ja get dem boots, bro?" came a voice from behind me. "You get dem at da Warehouse?" (The Warehouse is New Zealand's answer to Liquidation World.)

I turned around and found several of the young Mongrel Mob wannabes checking out my boots. I took note of their tattoos and white, grungy abattoir boots. They had spied my Sorels and were keenly interested. Those Sorels must have looked like the ultimate in gang attire. Not only were they white, but they were also lined. They must have looked far more inviting than those cold, gummy things.

It didn't take me long to realize that because of the Maori fondness for "borrowing," my treasured white Sorels would magically disappear by the time I returned to put them back on. I didn't fancy returning home barefoot so that my Sorels could become some wannabe gang member's claim to fame. In a daring act of cultural ignorance, I kept the boots on and slept in them—rather comfortably, I might add—on the floor of the freezing *marae*.

Those Sorels did end up staying in New Zealand when our family returned to Canada. We moved back to British Columbia the following year, culturally enriched and financially unburdened. I sold my ski jacket and Sorel boots later that winter to a nice, effeminate fellow who worked at the ski rental shop at the top of the Whakapapa ski hill. I didn't fancy lugging them home. In the end, I got more than I had paid for them in money, mileage, and memories.

Karen Lewis loves to travel and is currently trying to earn her "certificate of world citizenship." When she's not teaching English and Comparative Civilizations at an Okanagan high school, she loves visiting the ski slopes around Rossland, BC. She currently lives with her family in Kelowna.

Freeze Frame

Where you travel is sometimes less important than who you travel with.

By Jennifer Ball

The Canadian Prairies may be famous for their frigid winters and endless vistas, but they also deserve recognition for their spectacular summer storms. As a girl who grew up on an Alberta farm, I was always fascinated by these blitzkriegs of Prairie weather.

Sometimes it's almost as though night swoops down on you in the middle of the day. One minute you might be basking in glorious sunshine, and the next you'll find yourself in the middle of a downpour. After years of experience you start to recognize the earthy smells that precede these fast-moving black blankets of weather, but you never stop being awed by their beauty and power. Of all the Prairie seasons, it is the season of the thunderstorm that beguiles me the most.

Our family spent a lot of time travelling around Alberta during the summer months, after my father had finished seeding and before the harvest began. My mom, you see, was a fanatical collector of lapel pins; it was her personal mission to collect pins from every hamlet, town, and village in Alberta—and she personally drove to every one of them to make her purchase! My father and mother were true kindred spirits, and he would often humour her obsession by good-naturedly making pin-collecting detours to colourful little places like Nanton, Pincher Creek, and Drumheller. On those occasions when he couldn't come, he always looked forward to hearing about her latest find, which she would then add to our "walk of fame" hallway where all the pins were displayed.

I remember vividly one summer road trip that I took with my mom and her best friend Rosie. We had spent the day poking around several small towns east of Strathmore and I was riding in the back doing what I did best as a seventeen-year-old: eavesdropping on front-seat, grown-up conversations and staring out the window.

We were getting close to Strathmore on our way home when a summer storm blew in. This storm seemed particularly violent, and my heart raced as the thunder boomed and the sky repeatedly split apart.

I looked down at my mom's camera on the seat beside me. It was a very expensive and sophisticated camera that I was rarely allowed to touch. I picked it up and looked up into the rearview mirror at my mom.

"Do you want to make a bet?" I asked.

She looked back at me with her famous goofy grin. "About what?"

"I bet I can photograph the lightning."

Like many seventeen-year-olds, I still possessed many innocent, childlike qualities, especially the endearing trait of believing that I was always right. I waited patiently for her response, but she just chuckled.

"Jennifer," she said. "That is two-hundred-speed film. It's dark out and we're in a moving car. You won't be able to take a picture of the lightning."

In my head I processed all the reasons she had just laid out, then convinced myself that these were mere distractions for a determined girl with a photographic eye. After all, I reasoned, my mom and I often went on hikes to the Red Deer River, where I watched her take simple but beautiful pictures of flowers and trees. How hard could it be to take a great picture of the lightning from a car moving at a hundred kilometres per hour, under a blackened sky, in a colossal downpour?

"Can I at least try?" I begged. "Please?"

I really wanted to show her that I was a chip off the ol' block.

When she reluctantly said, "Yes," I positioned myself next to the window and began snapping feverishly. The thunder rumbled ominously across the fields, its frightening claps making it hard for me to press the shutter to capture the next bolt. But I persisted.

Eventually my mom intervened, accusing me of wasting her precious film. Through the viewfinder it had looked like she was right, but deep inside I knew that one of those pictures would turn out. The storm passed and we were soon on our way home, talking about the great day we'd just had poking around some quirky southern Alberta towns.

Two days later my Mom brought home the developed film. As she rifled through the photos, I overheard her say, "I don't believe it ..."

In her hand was exactly what I'd seen through the viewfinder that evening—lightning streaking and popping across the inky sky. It didn't matter that all but one of those pictures were black, for in her hand she held a single, spectacular frame of a prairie sky splintered with shafts of lightning ... frozen for eternity.

Today, with years of photographic experience under my belt, I will acknowledge that there are better pictures of lightning. But none comes with a memory as fond as mine. That picture now hangs in our family farmhouse, blown up into an eight-by-ten print and framed. Any person who comments on it will hear the story behind my famous photo.

Apart from the taking of that picture, the story is really just a simple tale of one of the many great road trips I took with my mom. She truly loved the simple, rolling beauty of the Canadian Prairies, and never understood why I felt the urge to travel to faraway places when I had such staggering beauty in my own backyard.

That was one of the last pin-collecting road trips I ever took with my mom, who passed away suddenly six years later at the age of forty-four. Our family was devastated, yet that simple memory continues to put a smile on my face and fill my heart with joy.

In the year that followed, we all made peace with our memories of my mother, a loving and free-spirited woman who was perhaps the world's most enthusiastic pin collector. Many years before she got sick, she and my dad made a pact that if anything should happen to one of them, the other would join them in their favourite place: on the quiet shores of Buffalo Lake. And it was at this lake, while walking along the beach on a warm spring day the following year, that my father passed away, too. He was forty-eight.

I learned a lot from my Mom about appreciating the wonders of nature and enjoying the simple things in life. Some of our most memorable conversations took place in the car while we toured the back roads of Alberta. Most of the time she wouldn't even plan where we were going; we would just end up somewhere.

I have always appreciated my family and the times we spent together, but the passing of my parents at such a young age has reinforced this all the more. That picture of a lightning bolt sizzling across a black Prairie sky stands frozen in my mind—one small yet poignant symbol of memories that will last a lifetime.

Jennifer Ball prides herself on blowing every penny she earns on travel, both in Canada and to exotic destinations abroad. In recent years the pennies have been much fewer as she's stayed home to raise her two beautiful boys, an experience that even the rigours of international travel couldn't have prepared her for. Jennifer currently lives with her family in the concrete jungle of Red Deer, Alberta.

Hungry

A day of endurance in Southeast Asia.

By Russell & Penny Jennings

W̲e froze.

A strange noise had woken us. Someone was in the room.

It was early morning, still pitch black. I felt for the flashlight on the chair by the bed and shone it at the table.

A cat! It leapt onto the windowsill, squeezed between the steel security bars, and disappeared.

We were relieved it was only a cat. I was now wide awake, so I checked my watch. Five o'clock. We decided to get up and eat, as we had an early train to catch.

"Where's our loaf of bread?" Penny asked. "It was on the table last night." We searched the room and discovered leftover hunks of bread on the windowsill and the floor. The cat had stolen our breakfast!

My wife and I were staying in the Government Rest House, a hotel in the northern Bangladesh town of Panchagarh. Not far away was a convenient border post we planned to cross to reach Darjeeling in northern India. The previous day, however, a Bangladeshi customs official had advised us against crossing in the north. According to him, the Bangladeshi officials would allow us to cross the border, but the Indian officials would not permit us to enter India because of civil unrest in the area. He had suggested we take the next morning's six-thirty train via Dinajpur to Biral, a border post to the southwest of Panchagarh.

We packed our belongings and in the semi-darkness strode to the town square, hoping to replace our breakfast. But it was too early for bread shops to be open or street vendors to be selling food. In the town square we spotted a lone rickshaw with the driver curled up on the seat. He lived in his rickshaw, as so many of them did. Penny gently shook his shoulder; we didn't want to disturb his sleep, but with our heavy packs, we did need a ride. He rubbed his eyes and smiled, pleased to get work so early in the day.

He pedalled quietly through the empty streets to the train station. Only the crunch of rickshaw tires on the gravel road broke the stillness. Being on the streets of a town before it wakes up evokes a special calming effect on a person. The silence was a pleasant contrast to the ringing of bicycle bells, the honking of car horns, the calls of vendors appealing to customers, and all the other sounds made by people scurrying in every direction as they do in Asian cities.

We caught the train at six-thirty. There had been no time to search for food, so we sustained ourselves for the next four hours on two thermos flasks of water and a few candies.

The train station in the border town of Biral consisted of a platform and a small office building. People stared at us curiously, as though we were oddities. We guessed that few travellers used this route.

The stationmaster and two government officials led us into the Customs and Immigration room, which was furnished with a table and a half-dozen chairs. A young boy came in and grabbed a rope that was attached to a rectangular carpet suspended from the ceiling—a *pankha*, or hanging fan. As he pulled the rope, the carpet swished back and forth, stirring the humid air. The young fellow was a *pankhawallah*, whose job it was to keep the officials cool.

The only light in the room came from the doorway and a single small window. But they were soon blocked by the heads of curious men and boys who crowded around outside the building, all craning their necks to see the two foreigners in their midst. The senior official told us that the last foreigners to cross the border at Biral were a Dutchman six months earlier and a German traveller one year before him. Biral was normally only used by Bangladeshi and Indian traders, the stationmaster added.

The senior official checked our passports for Bangladeshi visas, but was baffled when he found a visa in my passport but not in my wife's. I explained patiently that Penny did not need a visa, being a Canadian, but I needed one, being an Australian. After deliberating with the other two men and shaking his head, the senior official told us we would have to return to Benopal in the south (where we had entered Bangladesh) and leave by that same border post. I objected, saying it was not possible, and argued that the Dutchman and the German had passed through.

I couldn't imagine retracing our steps just because these officials were unsure how to process our documents.

The junior official took the initiative and searched for something in a cupboard. He finally found it—the little-used register. He placed the oversized book on the wooden table, flipped through the pages of our passports, and picked up a pen to enter our names, nationalities and passport numbers. His writing was painstakingly slow as he formed each letter and number with precision. Still, I was relieved to see some positive action.

Junior now needed the Departure stamp. He looked in the drawer. Not there. He went to the cupboard that was piled with account books, stacks of dog-eared papers, and a jungle of rubber stamps that had been gathering dust for years. Not there either. Eventually he found it, blew the dust off, inked a dry stamp pad, and with a flourish, stamped our passports. The whole exercise took an hour and a half.

Now we were officially out of Bangladesh.

I turned to the stationmaster. "What transport can we get to the Indian border town?"

"There is nothing," he replied. "The train line between Bangladesh and India is not used anymore. It is a six-mile walk."

"We could go by ox cart," Penny suggested.

"The farmers don't go that far. You'll have to walk," he said. "But it is too hot right now; wait until it cools down. The Indian train leaves at four from the border."

It was now midday. The sun was blazing down on us, but we were determined to catch that train. We filled our thermos flasks with boiled water (to kill the bacteria) at the train station and slung our backpacks over our shoulders. Spotting a street vendor, we bought his last packet of crackers, then started along the disused railway track.

The countryside around us was flat, brown, parched, and inhospitable. We passed by a small village of square, squat mud-brick huts packed tightly together like pieces of a jigsaw puzzle. Curious men and women looked up from their garden plots and stared. Children screamed and took refuge indoors.

Penny looked at me. "If we're only the third and fourth Westerners in eighteen months to pass this way, we may be the first Westerners the children have seen."

I nodded agreement. "With our big backpacks, we must look as if we're from another planet."

Beyond the village, the terrain stretched to the horizon like a crumpled brown carpet. The sun pursued us with relentless ferocity, its heat oppressive and dry like a blast of air from the open door of an oven. Every ten minutes we stopped to rest and sip water from our diminishing supply. After a further half-hour of trudging in the heat we arrived at the rim of a gulch with a river of reddish-brown water curling below. The steep slope down to the river was sparsely vegetated with clumps of hardy grasses and scrub, but not enough to stop erosion of the reddish-brown earth.

Spanning the gulch was a wooden trestle bridge more than a hundred feet long and thirty feet above the river. This was a challenge I hadn't expected. The railway tracks ran over metal ties spaced widely apart. To step from one tie to the next we would have to stretch our legs to the maximum. Between the ties was nothingness—a space big enough to fall through.

Penny turned to me, eyes wide open in fright. "I can't cross that," she blurted. "My legs won't stretch that far and I can't stand heights."

I was nervous too, so I scanned up and down the river for a possible place to ford. But it looked too deep.

"We have to cross the bridge," I said. "There's no other way. I'll hold your hand."

Penny hesitated, looked up and down the river for a crossing point, then agreed to tackle the bridge.

We set off. I looked down between the ties and saw the deep brown river. A lump formed in my throat, and my heart skipped a beat. "Try not to look down," I told Penny as I gripped her hand tighter, not only to reassure her but to boost my own nerve.

At each step, we stretched our legs in rhythm to the next tie. About a third of the way across, I noticed that her knees were knocking. It was too late to go back. I stopped for a breath and looked around at the pastry-coloured landscape. We were two cherries on top of a baking pie.

"Let's not stop," said Penny as she wavered on a railway tie. "If we do, I'll lose my balance."

"If we fall," I said, "we have to slip our backpacks off before hitting the water so we won't get dragged under."

Penny's legs suddenly wobbled uncontrollably. Had I said something wrong? "Relax," I told her. "Try to stay calm."

"I'll be all right. I can do this."

"You're doing fine."

As we continued, Penny's backpack suddenly shifted. She tightened her grip on my hand and I struggled to keep my balance. Adrenaline rushed through my veins. I stopped, breathed deeply, and waited until the butterflies in my stomach had folded their wings again.

I glanced over at Penny, who was taking quick, shallow breaths. "Breathe deeply," I said. With great difficulty, she slowed her breathing.

At each step, I coaxed both of us forward. "Stretch your leg farther. You're doing great. Now, another step. Not far to go. Keep up the rhythm. We're nearly there. Just one more step." Then finally, "We've made it!"

Penny's legs had turned to rubber. She collapsed onto the ground, emotionally and physically a wreck. I didn't feel too great myself. We sat for a while to rest and regain our strength, but we couldn't escape the burning sun. Our water was running low and we only had a few candies left. The crackers we'd bought were stale and inedible.

"How far do we still have to go?" Penny asked.

I wasn't sure. We'd been walking for three hours. "Maybe two more," I replied hopefully.

A grove of trees appeared in the haze ahead of us. We hoped we were nearing the station, but as we got closer, the trees faded away—they were a mirage.

Finally, after rounding a curve, we saw a shimmering building far ahead and tried to quicken our pace. It must be the train station. Or another mirage.

Then, in the distance, we saw puffs of black smoke rising in the blue sky. Then we heard the faint whistle of a train. It was leaving right on time: four o'clock. We were late.

We staggered into the station, so exhausted that we collapsed on the platform. I was vaguely aware that several people had gathered around us. After a short rest we looked around and found a water tap. We splashed water onto our faces to cool down, but we didn't dare drink it. We had been so careful to purify our water during our travels that we didn't want to take a chance and drink carelessly.

The stationmaster, a tall stoop-shouldered man, appeared and told us the next train was at seven. He also said that an immigration official would come to inspect our documents. At dusk the official arrived, carrying a coal-oil lamp. He was a skinny man of about thirty-five with nicotine-stained teeth and fingers. He thumbed through our passports. "Where are your visas for India?" he asked in a gruff voice.

"We don't need visas for India," I replied calmly.

"Do you have a permit to enter India at this border control?" he asked. We presented our Darjeeling Entry Permit. It expired that day, and although it had nothing to do with this border control, we hoped it would satisfy him.

He glanced at the permit with a disapproving grimace and tried to make a telephone call. Whoever he was calling wasn't there. He appeared unsure what to do with us and seemed to be relieved when the stationmaster and an assistant arrived. They discussed what they should do in loud, animated voices, replete with lots of arm waving. Then the official tried to make another call. Still no luck.

He asked where we had been and where we were going, then took a large book from a shelf, blew off the dust, and as I explained, started writing. He peered at Penny's passport in the dull light of the lantern, puzzled because Penny's maiden name appeared along with her married name and her three given names.

He was a slow writer. About an hour later, he finished recording our details in the book, then finally took the rubber stamp out of the desk drawer and stamped our passports with a thump.

Now we were officially in India.

The whistle blew as the seven p.m. train entered the station. We were the only passengers getting on. We stretched out on the seats, our empty stomachs grumbling piteously, thankful to at least be horizontal. But even that grace only lasted fifteen minutes. At the next stop throngs of people poured through the doorways. Some even climbed through the windows.

After a long, crowded, sleepless five hours, we arrived at the town of Katihar. We were tired, hungry, and thirsty. It was midnight, but the dark streets were noisy and crowded with people meeting the train, and others haggling for rickshaws. We were about to look for a hotel when a man appeared out of the darkness and said he would take us to one around the corner. Whether he was just a helpful bystander or a representative of the hotel, we never found out. It was not unusual for people to materialize from nowhere, offer help when needed, then fade away.

The Hotel Ashok was mostly used by train travelers with next-day connections. Our small room had a ceiling fan, a small side table, and two *charpoys*—beds with mattresses made of woven rope. Our noses told us the toilet and shower were down the hall.

At the check-in desk, I asked the clerk if there was anywhere we could get some food and boiled water. He offered to bring something.

He returned with bowls of meat in sauce, stale *chapattis*, and a large bottle of beer. I tasted the meat and sauce. *Yikes!* It was *Spicy!* It shot me into orbit, scorched my tongue, and sizzled my amalgam fillings. I grabbed the beer and poured it down my throat to douse the fire in my belly.

Neither of us could eat the spicy food, nor the *chapattis*. Our thermos flasks had been filled with odd-tasting hot water that we weren't able to bring ourselves to drink. At the end of an exhausting day that had started twenty hours earlier with the sound of a noisy cat stealing our breakfast, we dozed off. Still hungry.

Russell and Penny Jennings connected in 1975 on a blind date. Since then, they have left their sandal prints in dozens of countries on six continents. One such place is India, where they stayed in zero-star hotels as they crisscrossed the country by train and foot. During their three-month odyssey, they gorged themselves on four hundred bananas each. Their home is Vancouver, where they ban bananas from their fruit bowl. Visit the Jennings online at **www.worldweatherguide.com**.

The Snowball Effect

Some travelling companions possess a momentum all their own.

By Nadine Dunseith

My boyfriend Bruce and I stood on the shoulder of the Trans-Canada Highway outside Calgary, our thumbs in the air. We were waiting patiently for that elusive first ride. Cars whizzed by and the stiff Prairie wind whipped at our hair. Bruce was holding a sign that read: WINNIPEG. That was our first stop, though we hoped to travel as far as Cape Breton Island to visit with my family on Canada's east coast.

A small camper van finally pulled over. The driver, a young fellow named Chris, told us that he would drive us to Strathmore, a town forty-five minutes east of Calgary. He offered to do this even though his destination was actually Lethbridge, a small city in southern Alberta. He didn't mind the detour, he explained. He had hitchhiked before and he knew what it was like to wait for a ride.

We found that we had a lot in common with Chris: we all shared stories about our tree-planting adventures, and Bruce and I told the tale of our spontaneous decision to embark on this cross-Canada hitchhiking journey. When we reached Strathmore, Chris suggested dropping us at a local truck stop; he said it was a good place to see if any long distance truckers would take us onboard. We were all enjoying our conversation, however, so we first sat down for a cup of coffee with him.

After finishing his coffee, Chris went to the men's room while Bruce and I walked over to some parked semi trailers to petition for a ride. Unfortunately, it soon became evident that nobody would take us, so we walked back to the restaurant and ran into Chris on his way out. When we told him we'd struck out, he got a peculiar look on his face and told us to sit down and wait.

"I'll be back in a moment," he said.

Bruce and I were curious about Chris's plan, so although we were prepared to continue thumbing it on the highway, we decided to wait. When Chris returned, he told us that his uncle Mike was leaving that day on a road trip from Calgary to Toronto, which meant he would be passing through Strathmore. Chris had tried phoning him at home (this was before the cellphone era), but there had been no answer. He suspected that his uncle had left already.

"But if we're lucky," he continued, "my uncle will be passing through Strathmore any moment now." Chris convinced us to wait with him at the side of the highway until we saw Mike drive by. We would then try to catch his attention by waving vigorously while honking Chris's horn.

Bruce and I were astounded. Chris's determination to secure us a ride seemed both genuine and absurd—of course we would give it a try!

The wait felt like an eternity as we watched hundreds of cars pass, but neither of us minded. We were intrigued to see where

Chris's idea would lead us—and more importantly, we were enjoying his company.

Suddenly, Chris spotted his uncle's car. He leaned on his horn, tooting it a dozen times or more, while Bruce and I frantically waved our arms. But his uncle didn't notice.

"Get in," said Chris. "I think we can still catch him."

Once we were safely inside, he roared onto the highway and started the pursuit.

The next fifteen minutes passed in a blur. As Chris tracked his uncle's vehicle, we found ourselves in the middle of a high-speed chase straight out of a Hollywood movie. After about fifteen minutes we caught sight of Mike's car again, and once we were a few dozen metres behind him, Chris again honked his horn. But it was to no avail—his uncle seemed oblivious.

Chris sped up and pulled into the passing lane. When we were directly parallel with his uncle's car, Chris hammered on the horn until Mike looked over. Chris motioned for him to stop; Mike looked perplexed, but he noticed it was Chris driving, so he pulled over onto the shoulder. Bruce and I waited in Chris's van while he and his uncle shared a few words.

It turned out that Mike was not the least bit upset or put out by his nephew's request. In fact, we soon discovered that Mike had already picked up two other hitchhikers, Jessie and Shane, who were on their way to Regina. It was a little cramped for those first nine hours, but we didn't mind. Mike proved to be the most considerate man we met on our hitchhiking adventure, and we learned a lot from him.

Mike was the most optimistic and positive person we had ever met; he instilled the belief in us that there is no such thing as "never." "It's too negative," he said many times.

He introduced us to his "personal power" tapes, and at one point, had the four of us take a personality test in which we each drew a house, a river, a snake, a pathway, and the sun. If we drew a house with a door and windows and a pathway leading to it, he said, we were friendly and open to new people in our lives. I felt this summed up Mike's own personality.

Mike even bought us breakfast a couple of times, and after we'd reached Toronto, he purchased a pair of transit tickets so we could reach our destination in one of the city's suburbs.

Although Bruce and I had initially embarked on our hitchhiking adventure to save money, it became so much more than a cost saving exercise. Meeting Mike and Chris in such an unexpected manner gave us the opportunity to open our minds to new ideas. And the many generous people we met on our trip strengthened our faith in humanity.

Snowballs start small and grow larger as they roll. Our hitchhiking adventure from British Columbia to Nova Scotia also started small, and grew more life-changing and meaningful with each new person we met and experience we had—a "snowball effect." Mike, Chris, and all the other people we met became a part of our lives for a brief period, yet our memories of them will last a lifetime.

Nadine Dunseith often peruses the dictionary for interesting and elaborate words. She is a subscriber to dictionary.com and a fan of Jeopardy. She hopes to one day become an acclaimed writer, but first she would love to appear as a Jeopardy contestant so she can dominate the category "Books and Authors." In her spare time she marks papers for her Language Arts classes.

Hinterland Honeymoon

Are we having fun yet?

By Matt Jackson

Stop. Before you read any further, take a few moments to imagine the perfect honeymoon destination.

Take a deep breath…

Fold your hands in your lap…

Now close your eyes and let your thoughts carry you away…

Okay, open your eyes again. What did you see? Does your vision of honeymoon paradise involve a five-star hotel, a beach with white talcum-powder sand, gourmet food, plenty of sunshine, and palm trees bowing gently under a sea breeze?

Or maybe you'd prefer a luxury rail tour through Europe. Can you taste that Swiss chocolate? Smell those French pastries? *Magnifique!*

In the months leading up to our wedding, my fiancée and I were confronted with these and other choices regarding our honeymoon. In the end, we opted for something a little different: a two-week, hundred-kilometre trek across Baffin Island's Auyuittuq National Park. We read some online brochures about it, made some phone calls, and just couldn't resist the thought of honeymooning in the Arctic wilderness while sleeping in a leaky tent and humping overstuffed backpacks across rugged, trail-less terrain. The clincher? Realizing that every couple hundred metres we would get to stop and nervously scan the horizon for marauding polar bears.

The bazillion bloodthirsty mosquitoes were just an unexpected bonus.

*   *   *

With the ink barely dry on our marriage certificate, my wife Stacey and I arrived in the tiny Inuit community of Qikiqtarjuaq on Baffin Island's north shore. It was early August, but the harbour was still packed with "bergy" bits—truck-sized chunks of glacier ice that had calved off Greenland's icecap, then drifted on ocean currents along Baffin's chiselled shoreline until they got snagged against Broughton Island.

We met another couple onboard our flight: Jean-Yves, a charismatic French Canadian fellow from northern Ontario, and happy-go-lucky Christine, from southern Alberta. They were working as teachers in Yellowknife—capital of the Northwest Territories, and Canada's northernmost capital city—but they had never travelled above the Arctic Circle. The road-less wilderness of Auyuittuq had been calling them just as it had us.

We spent the afternoon walking around Qik (pronounced *kick*), passing classically red, octagonal stop signs that were emblazoned with Inuktitut characters. Most of the town's buzzing ATVs seemed to disregard them anyway. Many of the homes had orange Arctic char fillets hanging from their porches; some had whalebone ornaments; yet others featured drying seal skins stretched across wooden frames.

"I feel like we're in a different country," Stacey remarked as we walked along the beach adjacent to Qik's harbour. Our new friends whole-heartedly agreed.

That night we played cards together in a luxury Airstream trailer—our one-night retreat before the hard work began. We knew the north shore of Baffin was the most likely place we would encounter a hungry polar bear—the bears hunt for seals while riding the ice floes off the shore—and for that reason Stacey and I thought strength in numbers would improve our collective odds. We asked the other couple if they wanted to spend the first couple of days hiking together.

"Are you sure that's all right with you?" asked Christine. "We don't want to impose on your honeymoon."

"You're not imposing," Stacey insisted.

"If we don't like each other after two days," I added, using my most charming voice, "we can always ditch each other."

We left Qikiqtarjuaq at around eleven the following day, dressed in baggy, bright orange floatation suits that made us look like sunburned Michelin Men. A flawless blue sky promised continuation of the good weather, but it also meant choppy sea conditions. Nevertheless, we were treated to a fine spectacle. As our water taxi slalomed through the drifting pack ice, the sheer walls of Baffin's fjords reared up in all directions, hinting at the imposing wilderness we would spend the next two weeks hiking through.

We didn't arrive in the park until well after four. On top of that, our water taxi driver came down with a condition known as *lazyitis*, and opted to leave us several kilometres north of the designated drop-off location. To ensure against polar bear encounters, Parks Canada recommends that hikers walk as far inland as possible on their first day; this unexpected add-on meant we would be in the "danger zone" longer than we had planned.

As the driver prepared to leave, he fished something out of his cooler and threw it ashore, perhaps in an attempt to make us feel better. A large slab of meat landed on a shoreline rock at our feet.

"What is that?" I asked.

"Muktuk," the man said. "It's whale blubber. I forgot to let you try it on the trip out here." He unsheathed his hunting knife and sliced off a small piece for each of us. It was a narwhal, he said, and he told us to eat the grisly morsel fur and all. To me it tasted like a hairy piece of gristle, but I managed to choke it down and smile as I did so. Out of respect for the man's Inuit culture, the others did the same.

As the driver was getting ready to push off again, I reminded him to take the rest of the muktuk with him. "That's fine," he said cheerily. "You can take the rest of it with you. I'm sure you'll be hungry later today."

Jean-Yves and I looked at each other nervously. The driver had dropped us several kilometres north of the park boundary—which we didn't mind too much, as long as we didn't run into a polar bear—but our packs were already heavy enough. The last thing we wanted to carry was an extra two pounds of polar bear bait.

"No, you can take it back," Jean-Yves insisted.

"Really, it's no problem," the man repeated, smiling. "It's my gift to you."

In the end, all of us were able to save face. The taxi driver motored away, content that he had been a generous host, and soon disappeared around a shadowy corner of the fjord. Then Jean-Yves kicked the whale blubber into the sea.

*   *   *

"Oh my God…" I said nervously as I focused the telephoto lens of my camera. I was training it on a large white object Christine had spotted a few hundred metres up the valley.

Three gasps came from behind me.

"What is it?" Jean-Yves finally managed.

"Oh my God…" I repeated. I turned around and fixed my companions with a broad grin. "…it's a *big white rock!*"

"Geez, Louise!" said Christine. "Don't scare us like that."

Stacey swatted my shoulder. "You're such a brat," she said.

Geez, Louise was right. Less than a week into our marriage and I was already suffering physical abuse.

It took us almost four hours to hike eight kilometres inland from where the water taxi had dropped us. We avoided encounters with any polar bears, but were fast falling prey to an equally bloodthirsty predator: the ubiquitous mosquito.

All the information we'd gathered about Auyuittuq before our trip had mentioned little about biting insects. For that reason, Stacey and I had simply assumed the extreme northern climes—or perhaps the relentless wind that funnels down off the nearby Penny Icecap—would make it impossible for mosquitoes to thrive. We knew there would be some, of course, but we hadn't thought they would be as severe a problem as they are in other parts of northern Canada. Our backpacks were already bulging at the seams, so we had decided to leave our high-tech bug jackets at home.

In Qik, we met a park patrol that had given us some bad news: the Owl River Valley at the north end of the park was teeming with mosquitoes. So we walked to the local co-op as fast as our little legs would carry us, and were relieved to find a pair of cheap bug nets available for purchase.

These tiny mesh nets, which we bought for the paltry sum of $1.50 each and wore over our heads, undoubtedly saved us from several days of misery. The supposedly omnipresent Arctic wind was nowhere to be found during the first three days, and the mozzies were out in droves. We ended up wearing our bug nets practically all day—as we walked, ate, drank, napped, did yoga, and whenever we felt moved to utter profound exclamations of joy (and the occasional bug-induced profanity) into the great Arctic emptiness.

Apart from the bugs, the walking also proved to be a challenge, despite the flat terrain and lack of bushwhacking. The Owl Valley was covered in a thick layer of soft sphagnum tussocks (mounds of moss) for much of its length. Walking across this layer of tussocks while hefting a seventy-pound pack is roughly equivalent to walking on a partially inflated air mattress for several kilometres with a refrigerator strapped to your shoulder blades.

Fortunately, we had a landscape of superlatives to keep us distracted.

Beneath the towering granite walls of the fjord we felt like ants. Icefields were draped over distant peaks, and glaciers snaked out of many of the side valleys like forked lizard tongues. Each morning we would get up and admire the expansive view, drink some coffee, slurp back several packets of instant oatmeal, and then dutifully check our map. We would then pick a landmark a short distance up the valley and agree to stop for lunch when we had reached it. However, such is the scale on Baffin that we generally wouldn't get there until two days later.

Baffin seemed larger than life.

*   *   *

Camped at the foot of Akshayuk Pass, we awoke to cold and penetrating drizzle on the morning of day six. Baffin gets a lot of precipitation during the summer months, and after our first day of sunshine, it had been raining on and off for the last four days.

Of course, lying in a warm, dry tent as the thrumming of rain patters against its outer shell can be wonderful—as long as there's no urgency to pack and leave camp. We had awakened to rain the previous morning, and after huddling to eat breakfast in the lee of the Glacier Lake emergency shelter—one of several small, wood-framed shelters along our route—we had voted to take a rest day.

After a short hike to the Rundle Glacier, we had used the "emergency shelter"—described as such because hikers are not supposed to use it except in emergencies—for several "emergency" games of cards: Hearts, Euchre, and a game Jean-Yves taught us called Screw Your Neighbour. Later, we had laughed over some emergency stories and enjoyed an emergency nap, all within the dry and cozy confines of the small shelter.

But this was day six and it was time to pack up and leave. We reluctantly crawled from our nylon domicile into a thick, Scotch mist. The mountains had disappeared overnight, the glaciers were hidden, and even the Owl River—a mere twenty metres from our tent—was barely visible. The morning felt like cold steel on bare skin, and we shivered as we packed up our soggy gear.

Once we were ready to go, the first order of business was crossing the Owl River, one of seven or eight fast-flowing, glacier-fed rivers that backpackers have to ford during the hundred-kilometre traverse. The Owl is one of the deepest crossings along the route and is by far the widest. It braids and meanders across a wide gravel plain below Akshayuk Pass, dividing into about a dozen channels hikers must negotiate to reach the other side. Several hikers have drowned while crossing rivers in the national park, which is why wardens recommend fording the deepest rivers early in the morning, when meltwater flow is generally at its lowest.

Trudging through the cold fog, we stumbled to the edge of the river and lily-dipped our toes into the murky water.

"Brrrrrrr!" said Christine. "That's bloody freezing!"

"This is going to get ugly," murmured Jean-Yves.

As the tallest in the group, it was my job to probe the deepest channels to make sure they were safe for the others. With hiking boots dangling around my neck to keep them dry, I plunged ahead in sandal-clad feet, wading into the opaque glacier melt.

Wet boots are not pleasant to hike in, which is why we repeatedly sacrificed our feet in this manner. With every channel we crossed, our bare feet and calves were dunked into swift-flowing glacial water that was only a fraction of a degree above freezing. After a few seconds of submersion it feels like tiny needles are being jabbed into your skin; a full minute and your feet go completely numb. It's not unlike the acute throbbing sensation of a gradually reawaking limb after you've been sitting on it for too long, only it happens to both feet simultaneously. By the time we had forded the Owl's dozen channels, it felt like our feet were encased in blocks of ice.

How serious is the sub-zero temperature of these glacier-fed rivers? We would later learn our lesson firsthand. Preferring extra stability, Stacey chose to ford the Owl in her hiking boots. When we reached the far side she didn't have to change footwear, so she simply kept her boots on, figuring her feet would warm up as we continued hiking. They never did warm up, however, and when we pitched camp that evening, she still couldn't feel the large toe on her left foot.

As her loving husband who only days before had committed my lifelong service to her wellbeing, I took the initiative and offered to amputate the offending digit with my Swiss Army knife. She graciously declined. I then suggested making a hot water bottle and sticking it with her feet inside a sleeping bag, which is exactly what we did. Over the next hour, her toe gradually regained its feeling.

A couple of weeks after we arrived home, however, her toe wrote its own epilogue: the nail turned charcoal-black and promptly fell off.

*   *   *

We spent the next three days traversing Akshayuk Pass—the highest point in the park—along the north shores of Glacier and Summit Lakes. This is the most rugged section of the hiking route, thanks mainly to the craggy and convoluted shorelines of the lakes, as well as multiple glacial moraines that we had to scramble up and over. Instead of the sponge-like meadows of the Owl Valley, we now found ourselves hiking over a chaotic jumble of wet and slippery boulders, which required a delicate sense of balance to negotiate with heavy packs on.

The views, however, were pure rapture. As dense fog moved in and out of the pass, snaggletooth spires would appear one moment, only to disappear the next as clouds swirled back into place. Waterfalls hundreds of metres high plunged from hanging glaciers, while tarns the colour of sapphires seemed to glow from within whenever a stray beam of sunlight struck them at just the right angle. It felt like a place drawn from Norse mythology, which is perhaps not surprising, in that we caught occasional glimpses of the park's most famous peaks: Thor and Asgard.

Our favourite campsite of the trip was on a narrow peninsula along the shores of Glacier Lake, practically at the foot of Mount Asgard and the Turner Glacier. The pass often acts as a wind funnel, so it's commonly a very windy place. But on the morning we awoke there, the fog had dissipated and the lake was dead calm, a perfect mirror reflecting the surrounding panorama. For many long minutes we sat contentedly on the lakeshore, sipping hot coffee and drinking in the view.

Awed by this smorgasbord of fine scenery, we soon felt compelled to capture the moment in a fitting manner. We set the self-timer on Stacey's digital camera, arranged ourselves carefully, and just before the shutter clicked, the four of us—in unison—dropped our drawers and mooned the camera.

It was, after all, our honey*moon*.

*　　*　　*

The rain continued falling for the last few days of our trek, with the exception of one glorious morning after we awoke in the shadow of Mount Thor's north face—the highest uninterrupted cliff face in the world. Thankfully, the hiking was much easier on the south side of Akshayuk Pass. Not only was there a well-used trail that led us down to South Pang Fjord—the terminus of our route—but we were quickly losing elevation. And for once, the ground we were walking on was solid and offered good purchase.

The wind was another matter. It picked up significantly on the south side of the pass to such an extent that one evening I actually felt compelled to build a one-metre rock wall surrounding the windward side of our tent. This may have prevented the heavy gusts from ripping our domicile from the ground, but it did nothing to stop the merciless thwacking of the nylon fly against the inside tent wall. It was like trying to sleep under a World War II artillery barrage.

On our last day, the four of us scrambled up a rocky slope for a view of the Tumbling Glacier, so named because it looks like the glacier is cascading down a nearby peak into Crater Lake. As we came down from our viewpoint, we met some other hikers on the trail, including a man and woman who were hiking with their four-month-old son. Mom was carrying the baby in a snuggly wrapped at her front, while Dad carried everything else (including diapers) in a single monstrous backpack.

"Out here for a few days?" I asked. Many visitors to the park start at the south end, hike in for a day or two, and then hike back out.

"No, we've been here for the last couple of weeks," the man said.

I was impressed. "Really? How far did you make it?"

"One of my friends is a warden here," replied the man. "We were up at Mount Asgard, trying to climb one of its ridge routes, but the weather never cleared for us." Mom and baby, of course, had stayed at base camp with another friend of the family. On their way back, just two days before, they'd successfully climbed Mount Thor.

Put in this comparative context, I guess honeymooning above the Arctic Circle isn't such a big deal after all.

Matt Jackson is the president of Summit Studios and author of the award-winning book The Canada Chronicles: A Four-year Hitchhiking Odyssey. *Despite the hardships of travelling in the far north, he and Stacey are planning a hiking and paddling trip to Alaska's Arctic National Wildlife Refuge in 2009.*

My Last Resort

When a vacation stops being a vacation.

By Lindsie Tomlinson Foreman

You know those times when you really need a vacation? When it doesn't matter where you go, as long as it's sunny and you don't have to think about work? When the biggest decision you want to make is whether to lounge at the pool or at the beach?

Well, my friend Teena and I were both feeling the need for just such a getaway. We decided to visit the Dominican Republic for a one-week stay at an all-inclusive resort, with a side trip to visit my sister, who was living there at the time.

It was a warm, sunny, beautiful afternoon when we arrived. Palm trees lined the beach, and the sound of the surf excited our senses while inducing that serene, magical state that only the ocean can bring on. Our hotel had a pool with a swim-up bar, a disco, and even a trapeze! Our room was a little older and what you might generously call "well used," but the location was perfect and the amenities were wonderful.

We fell immediately into vacation mode, donning our bikinis and retiring to the beach for an afternoon siesta, followed by dinner at a gorgeous open-air restaurant. After the meal, we relaxed on two of the oversized couches that were scattered randomly throughout the open-air lobby. There's nothing quite like wearing your summer wardrobe in a place that's warm—especially at midnight—knowing that in your hometown everyone is still wearing sweaters and jackets. Ah, the tropics!

When we woke the next day, we were disappointed to see clouds in the sky and rain falling outside our window. But it wasn't cold, so we dressed in bikini tops and shorts for a wet walk along the beach. Proud of ourselves for starting our day with some exercise, we ended up walking for a good ninety minutes before returning to our room so that we could change out of our wet clothes.

Did you know that you can get a wicked sunburn even if you can't see a ray of sunshine? Well, we didn't know. And yes, you can. And yes, I did.

My face and chest were a lovely shade of radiant red, and the burn on my chest was already breaking out in super-sexy blisters. These white bubbles contrasted beautifully with the bright red skin around them. In the lobby, a little girl actually pointed at my chest and cried to her parents, "What's that, mommy?"

On Day Two, my sister Sara picked us up so we could spend the weekend at her home in La Romana, an hour and a half away from our hotel in Punta Cana. Driving in the Dominican is an adventure. I don't know if there are any official rules of the road, but if there are, no one follows them. Unless the rules state to drive as fast and recklessly as possible, passing on either the left or the right (whichever you're in the mood for), while simultaneously honking your horn to indicate that you are about to do *something.* As in, *honk honk,* I'm going to pass you now! *Honk honk,* I'm turning left! *Honk honk,* I like the song you're playing in your car!

Many people travel by motorcycle, and sometimes an entire family crams onto one bike. It's not unusual to see three people riding on the same one: the mom, the dad, and their child. My sister once saw seven people on the same motorcycle—three adults and four children. You will also see people carrying everything from huge gas canisters to washing machines, pigs to small horses on the back of their bikes. Typically, one person drives while the passenger clutches the cargo tightly.

That night we went out for Mexican food, then paid a visit to a local disco where Sara's husband and his friends taught Teena and me three styles of dancing: salsa, merengue, and bachata.

Speaking of Mexican food … let me tell you about plumbing in the Dominican.

If you stick to the resorts and major restaurants, you will not experience Dominican plumbing. Real Dominican plumbing is nothing like what we are used to in North America. It's a bit of an adventure.

For one thing, you cannot throw toilet paper into the toilet without causing it to plug. You must throw your used toilet paper into the wastepaper basket (which seemed disgusting to me— but they do take the garbage out every day). If, like me, you are accustomed to tossing paper into the toilet, this new habit can be a very difficult thing to remember.

After dinner, I threw the toilet paper into the toilet.

The instant it left my hand, I remembered that I was not supposed to do this. What could I do? I wanted to flush and hope for the best, but as I reached for the handle, I realized I had no idea what might happen. Let's just say the possibilities unnerved me.

So I fished it out.

Not the most enjoyable thing to do after eating Mexican food. But better than dealing with an overflowing bowl of *El Crappo*.

Another thing I learned about Dominican plumbing is that hot water is a luxury. My sister Sara had this luxury, but there was a switch you had to flick to go from cold to hot. If you ran the hot water for more than thirty seconds at a time, it would blow the electricity for the entire building.

Needless to say, I washed and shampooed at top speed while counting backward from thirty.

My sister thought it would be fun to take us on a road trip to the capital city of San José, a five-hour drive from her place. She took us to see some caves, but along the way we were privileged to experience other sights we would have missed had we remained at our resort. Sights like a dead horse on the side of the road. Cows eating garbage in the street. And a mangy dog that appeared at every turn, no matter how far you drove. I could have sworn it was the same dog following us, but it turns out that most Dominican dogs look exactly like this one, with low-hanging teats from multiple litters of puppies.

I woke with a cold that day, and my congestion only increased the further we drove. Stopping for cold medicine and cough drops didn't help, and by the time we arrived at the home of my sister's in-laws, all I could do was crawl into bed while Teena received Spanish lessons from Sara's father-in-law.

I awoke the following day to find little bugs crawling all over the inside of my purse. They especially seemed to love my cough drops.

Still struggling to breathe through my nose, I left with Teena and Sara to go shopping in search of cheap cigars, rum, and coffee. My sister and I ended up getting into a big argument that ended in tears (hers) and silence (mine), plus confusion (her husband's) as he couldn't understand our rapid-fire English.

The drive back to our resort was tense. Teena and I sat in the back seat with John's brother, while Sara drove and John sat in the passenger seat. After a few awkward, silent hours, we stopped to make a left turn and were promptly rear-ended by a bus.

The driver didn't notice us until it was too late to brake or swerve, so he hit us at full speed. There was a deafening *crunch!* of twisting metal and breaking glass as we lurched forward. Only my seatbelt stopped me from flying through the windshield.

Miraculously, no one was seriously injured. Looking at that bus compared to our smashed-up little car, I found it hard to believe we hadn't all been killed.

There's nothing like getting hit by a bus to end an argument between sisters. Sara was quite shaken up, as she had been driving and no doubt would have felt responsible if anything had happened to us.

There was a police station nearby, so we cautiously started the car and drove there to file a report. The bus driver claimed to have no insurance and no license, so the police weren't going to let him leave until he produced some sort of documentation. The trunk of our rental vehicle was smashed in so far that we had to pry it open and rip off what remained of the bumper to get at our things. Incredibly, our cheap bottle of rum survived the crash; we found it wedged between the wheel well and the bent-in rear hatch.

The bus driver eventually produced some documentation and we were allowed to leave. Unbelievably, the car was still drive-able—we just had to pile our luggage on top of us in the back seat.

Back at our hotel, Teena and I spent the evening walking around in a daze, both feeling that we had somehow cheated death and were lucky to be alive. We were very sore and I could barely move my neck, but none of that really mattered. We were alive!

On our last evening before flying home, we enjoyed a delicious seafood dinner, which turned out to have some unexpected and unwelcome side effects. I spent the night in the bathroom throwing up and suffering horrible stomach cramps. The next morning I nearly missed our bus to the airport because I just couldn't keep anything down. Throwing up was the last thing I managed to do before suffering through a bumpy bus ride. It was also the first thing I did upon arriving at the airport.

That's when we learned about the airport's "In Case You've Somehow Survived the Dominican" tax. To leave the Dominican by air, all travellers are required to pay twenty US dollars (cash only) for the privilege of leaving the country. It was our own fault for not reading the fine print on the way in—but unfortunately, all we had left between the two of us was twenty Canadian dollars and a few Dominican pesos.

In a final act of desperation, we were forced to approach strangers and ask them for money. We felt like beggars. A fellow Canadian finally took pity on us and traded our twenty Canadian dollars for twenty US, and a tour agent agreed to buy our last few pesos so we could cover the rest of the fee.

At the airport in Vancouver, my boyfriend hugged me and told me that he was sorry to end my dream vacation on a sad note: a neighbour had just spotted his cat limping with what appeared to be a badly broken leg. After dropping Teena off at home, we found his cat, and I spent the rest of the evening at the veterinary clinic doubled over with stomach cramps and a badly peeling chest.

I've never been so happy to return home from a trip.

Lindsie Tomlinson Foreman is now married to said boyfriend. They are travelling around the world for a year trying not to get sunburned or sick in Thailand, Laos, Australia and Europe.

The Cadillac of Doom

Kids … don't try this at home.

By Benjamin Bowler

It's been said that the ones you love the most also hurt you the most. I once owned a 1991 Volkswagen GTI that consistently illustrated that sentiment.

I loved that car: it was sporty, fast … and more important, it looked cool. I affectionately christened it the Green Hornet, based on its colour. Yet despite my affections, mistrust plagued our relationship. In the months I owned that beautiful little speed machine, it consistently let me down and left me stranded at the side of the highway.

One frosty winter morning, the Green Hornet died on the road to Castle Mountain Ski Resort, which lies in southwestern Alberta roughly a hundred kilometres west of Lethbridge, where I was living at the time. I had been planning a day of snowboarding, but now that was shot. I had to be at work in Lethbridge the following day, so I employed my only option. I stuck out my thumb.

I easily hitched a ride to the base of the ski resort ten kilometres away, where I arranged for a tow truck to meet me at my car in an hour. However, catching a ride back to my car proved significantly more difficult. I glanced in anguish at my watch and power-walked frantically, praying I would make it in time for the rendezvous. There would be ample time if I managed to get a ride, but to cover ten kilometres on foot in one hour was impossible.

With my feet aching and time running out, I watched as a truck approached from the direction of my car and rolled down the window. "Is that your vehicle back there?" asked the bearded driver.

"Yeah," I said.

"Well, a tow truck is hooking it up right now," he said. "Get in, dude. If we hurry, we might be able to catch him."

With maneuvers that would have made any NASCAR driver proud, my redneck guardian angel delivered me just in time to catch the tow truck. I climbed in with the driver and rode to Pincher Creek, Alberta, a small ranching town three kilometres off Highway 3. Fortunately for me, Pincher Creek had a repair shop; unfortunately, this was a long weekend and it was closed.

The tow truck driver unhooked my car and I reluctantly deposited my keys into the mail slot of the empty service station. To get back home, I would have to continue hitchhiking.

I grabbed my snowboard and walked the three kilometres from the service station back to Highway 3, trying to remain optimistic that a ride home would soon materialize. But an hour of thumbing yielded nothing but frozen buttocks and a frosty disposition to match. I gave up and followed the icy highway back toward town, hoping to find an open gas station where I could buy a hot drink. Meanwhile, minivan after cursed minivan—without me inside—zipped past me on the highway.

It got better. When I finally reached a gas station, an enormous truck roared into the parking lot and nearly made me a hood ornament. The driver was a burly giant of a man named Rick, who was a railway worker from the Yukon. When I told him I was hitchhiking, he offered me a lift to British Columbia—which was roughly thirty minutes west and the opposite direction from home. I was stunned by the irony.

Then I had an idea. One of my snowboarding friends lived in a trailer park in Sparwood, a small town in British Columbia an additional half-hour or so west of the Alberta border. I decided to gamble on borrowing my friend's Pontiac Firenza to get home, so I accepted Rick's offer of a ride.

After Rick dropped me on the highway, a few more kilometres of cold and soggy walking placed me on the doorstep of the run-down trailer occupied by Dave "Dr. D.L." Lammle. It was empty, nobody was home, and no cars were parked outside.

By this time my desperation for a ride had taken a backseat to a more basic need—warmth. I was desperate. So while standing with one foot on his backyard barbecue, and with plenty of grunting and swearing, I managed to slide the kitchen window open, slither through the window (somehow avoiding a sink full of dishes), and land with a *thud!* on his kitchen floor.

With breaking and entering soon to appear on my rap sheet, I figured poaching a shower wasn't really pushing the envelope. While warming up and rinsing the day's stress away, I strategized my plan for getting home.

After drying off with a rather suspect facecloth, I poked my head out of the bathroom to find Dr. D.L. wide-eyed and wielding his snowboard like a battle-axe.

Standing in his hallway in my underwear, I have to admit feeling vulnerable. With my hands protecting my head, I explained the situation and inquired meekly about borrowing his car. He had purchased his mid-eighties Pontiac Firenza (with a camouflage paint job, no less) from another ski bum for a bottle of whisky a month earlier.

Unfortunately, my gamble came up snake-eyes when I learned that the Ferenza had neither insurance nor registration.

Dr. D.L. invited me to go snowboarding with him the next day at the nearby Fernie resort, suggesting with a trace of a smile that while it was illegal to drive to Fernie, it *had* snowed nearly twenty centimetres the night before—and prime snowboarding conditions like these might be considered extenuating circumstances. But I had to get home, so with a heavy heart I declined his offer.

So I found myself shivering on the shoulder of Highway 3 again, this time gripping a cardboard sign that read—no, *pleaded*—Lethbridge. With the sun long gone, the night took on an aching chill; aside from my snowboard, lonely thoughts and icy dragons of breath were my only company. I used my black Sharpie to amend my sign so it read Lethbridge *Please*. The highway wasn't as busy as it had been earlier in the day, but the odd car still passed as I stood beneath a streetlight hopefully displaying my cardboard placard. I stood there freezing for what seemed like an eternity, counting cars as they whizzed by.

About the time I felt I couldn't last even a minute longer, a new Cadillac streaked past. The brake lights flashed once and then glowed solid as the car slid to a sideways halt in the middle of the highway. The engine revved, and in one fluid motion the car spun a hundred and eighty degrees to face me. I heard the growl of the engine again and the spinning of the tires as the driver gunned it on the icy asphalt. The car blasted by me again, this time in the opposite direction, only to repeat the same hundred-and-eighty-degree rotation. As it drove toward me, I shielded my eyes from the headlights and searched for a place to dive out of the way. Then came the sound of crunching plastic as the Cadillac's front end hit an ice berm and it slid to a stop.

As I tried to decide whether this was a friendly encounter or not, the driver jumped out. He was middle-aged, but definitely did not look like your typical luxury car owner. He wore an AC/DC concert T-shirt and tight, tattered jeans with the knees torn out. A scrappy Camaro would have made sense, or even a rusted K-car, but certainly not a new Cadillac.

"Hitchhiking?" he asked as he circled the car toward me. Before I could answer, he cut me off. "Lethbridge *please*? Frickin' awesome! I've never seen a hitchhiker with a sign that says *please*. I had to stop."

Sensing that my night was about to get weird, I managed a feeble, "Right on, dude." I was desperate, and this ride was available. *Sure*, I thought, *the car is probably stolen, and the guy drives like a lunatic, but what's the worst that could happen?* My frozen toes encouraged me to find out.

Not wanting to damage the leather interior, I asked where to put my snowboard. "Throw it in the back seat," he laughed. "It's just a rental!"

Well, that explained a lot.

As I slid into the warm car and stowed my gear behind the driver's seat, the driver introduced himself as Steve, then pointed to a woman sitting next to him. "This is my sister," he explained. "She's from Nelson, and I'm giving her a ride to Calgary."

Apparently the woman had no name, though she did have a round, frizzy black Afro and dangling crystal earrings that grazed the shoulders of her green, knitted wool sweater. As I leaned forward in my seat to shake her hand, I noticed her long brown gypsy dress and Sorrel snow boots. Yep, she was definitely from Nelson.

Once the introductions were out of the way, I was slammed into my seat as Steve pinned the accelerator and fishtailed onto the highway. As he picked up speed, I tightened my grip on the seat's leather trim and felt the diameter of my sphincter decrease considerably. I released my grasp on the seat only momentarily to fumble for a seatbelt. This was not going to be the comfortable drive through the Crowsnest Pass that I had hoped for.

Before long, Steve was steering with one hand while rummaging through the Cadillac's center console. He glanced occasionally at the road to issue violent corrections, which invariably slammed me into the door. From the console he pulled an item that amplified my already white-knuckled grip on the seat: a Ziploc bag with several pre-rolled joints.

I had never wanted to be in a vehicle with a stoned driver—particularly with one who was blasting down an icy mountain road at night going twice the speed limit.

Now steering with his knee, while his foot remained firmly pinned to the accelerator, Steve twirled the end of a joint through a lighter's flame and blew on the tip until it burned evenly. Lifting it to his lips, he pulled a long drag of smoke deep into his lungs. He coughed and offered me a drag, which I respectfully declined. With a shrug, he took another hard pull and passed the joint to his sister. She seemed more than happy to smoke my share.

The taillights of a car appeared in the distance ahead, and as we closed the gap with shocking speed, Steve gave no indication that he might slow down. Surging forward, we drifted onto the shoulder of the highway. As the suspension vibrated across rumble strips, Steve summoned a loud "Whoooo!" and pushed the accelerator to the floor.

I took a shallow breath and felt the release of adrenaline surge through my veins. You know the terror is official when you can feel a pulse in your forehead; mine felt like a wrecking ball swinging into the sides of my skull.

We squeezed by within inches of the other car's passenger door. Through a window I saw the blurred silhouette of a middle finger.

Once we were past, the Cadillac suddenly jerked and slowed, causing the seatbelt to cinch tightly around my waist. I thought the Lord had heard my prayers and caused the car to malfunction.

"Governor," Steve informed me, explaining that the car had a mechanism that killed the engine once the vehicle accelerated past a hundred and eighty kilometres per hour.

I loosened my grip and slid my sweat-soaked back into the leather seat, thankful that someone had had the foresight to invent governors. But my relief was short lived. Before I could catch my breath, the engine revved again and Steve responded by slamming down the gas pedal.

"I'm going to die tonight," I murmured under my breath, but Steve and his sister were too stoned to notice.

The good news about driving fast is that it burns considerable amounts of fuel. Steve decided to stop for gas and a coffee in Blairmore, an idea I wholeheartedly endorsed. The drive between Sparwood and Blairmore takes approximately forty minutes in good weather. In bad weather, we covered it in twenty-five.

We pulled in beside the fuel pump, and with thankfulness in my heart, I opened the door and let my rubbery legs touch terra firma. I felt like throwing up.

While Steve bought coffee, I realized I had a decision to make.

Option One: Sever ties with Steve and the hippie and resume hitchhiking. This could lead to a slow, unglamorous death and I'd be found in the morning frozen in a snowbank.

Option Two: Continue this rolling gong show in the Cadillac of Doom and die like a rock star, my charred body discovered inside an overturned Cadillac beside a sign that read Lethbridge

Please. With the latter option, at least I'd die warm—and there was a chance, although slim, that I might get home in one piece.

I opened the Cadillac's door and nervously eased back into the seat.

For the next ten minutes Steve took it easy, sipping his coffee as he drove. I hoped the marijuana had mellowed his driving. The new, more reasonable speed pleased me considerably; I was going to make it home alive, or so I thought.

Then, as the lights of Bellevue shrank into the distance, it happened again. With a click, the center console opened and the bag of pot reappeared. The ritual of insanity resumed: Steve's knee to the steering wheel, the flick of the lighter, ignition, and lift-off. With the joint lit, the pedal hit the floor. I could barely see the highway through the cloud of smoke.

We kept up the breakneck pace for another fifteen minutes. With few cars on the highway, Steve managed to trigger the governor at regular intervals. Every time the engine cut, he would comment, "Cadillacs are bad-ass," to which the hippie would reply "Whoa!" This theatre of weirdness was like the Twilight Zone— Interior British Columbia edition. If an alien had jumped out of the glove box and eaten Steve and the hippie, it wouldn't have fazed me. In fact, at that point I would have invited it.

The "Bad-ass/Whoa" routine persisted until things went from bad to worse. An RCMP cruiser appeared on the road ahead.

"Cops!" I bellowed. The Cadillac slowed rapidly; this time it wasn't the governor. Steve had heard my desperate yelp from the back seat and swapped full throttle for hard brakes in an instant.

As we approached and passed the cruiser, the interior of the Cadillac was bathed in strobes of red and blue.

In that split second the Dynamic Doobie Duo unified into a task force. Windows were rolled down, the baggy of joints was stuffed into the console, and nostril-burning blasts of patchouli oil were fired into the interior to mask the smell of pot. These actions were reflexive, as though Steve and the hippy had trained extensively for that very moment.

This is it for me was all that went through my mind as we pulled over and the constable approached. *I am so screwed. Like meet-your-new-cellmate-named-Tiny screwed. Like being-traded-for-cigarettes-during-exercise-time screwed.*

There was absolutely no way an RCMP officer wasn't going to smell the pot on board, and even less chance he would believe the hitchhiking snowboarder in the back seat hadn't supplied the dope.

"License and registration please," said the officer. Then, incredulously, "Do you have any idea how fast you were going?"

"I'm sorry, officer," answered Steve. "I was drinking coffee and fooling around with the radio. Do you know you can't get any reception out here?" He continued rambling on. I sat silently with my head in my hands, trying not to be noticed.

Before Steve could finish, the cop cut him off. "One-forty. You were driving one hundred and forty kilometres per hour. Any idea what the speed limit is?"

"One-ten?" replied Steve coolly. Like a guru, he had transcended chemical influence and, in a moment of complete sobriety, transformed into a law-evading Jedi.

"Actually, it's seventy," said the officer. "That puts you at double the speed limit."

Between the fingers covering my eyes, I saw something that turned my stomach: the cop rested one hand on the door and leaned inside the window.

Despite Steve's respectable answers and the hippie's earlier blasts of fragrance, at this point I lost hope. We were doomed. The flashlight travelled back and forth over the floor of the car and over the dash, then flared in our wide eyes. None of us breathed.

"Stay here," said the officer. "I'll be back in a minute." He pulled his head out of the Cadillac and walked back to his cruiser, pausing to read the information on Steve's license plate.

The gravity of our situation began to sink in. Steve rolled up the window, ran his hands over his face and through his hair, and issued a deep sigh. "Do you guys think he smelled the bud?" he whispered out of the side of his mouth. I said nothing.

We waited, and then waited some more. It was torture. Finally, the constable appeared at the side of the Cadillac and knocked on the window.

"Okay sir," he said. "Here is what I've done for you. I've reduced your speed violation. The result is a fine of seventy dollars. It's your lucky night, so drive safe, and please *slow down*."

"Thank you, officer," said Steve. As he rolled up the electric window, the hum of its motor was the only noise in a breathlessly silent car. Steve and the hippie stared at each other, their gazes glazed over with confusion; then at me; then back to each other.

"I thought I was going to jail," said Steve through a goofy grin.

You very well could have, I thought to myself. *And probably should have.*

A few moments later, not wanting to test his luck, he pulled slowly onto the highway. Once he was certain the police car was out of range, he put the pedal down, but only until we reached a hundred and thirty kilometres an hour. At that point the speed was more than comfortable. After all I had been through, I could have gone to sleep.

At the town of Fort Macleod, just thirty minutes east of Lethbridge, Steve pulled the Cadillac into a parking lot. He and the hippie were going north to Calgary. This was where my ride ended.

Steve got out of the car and helped me pull out my gear. Standing silhouetted in the headlights, he produced a leather wallet, from which he slid a crisp business card. As he shook my gloved hand, he placed the card in my palm. It turns out that Steve was a real estate agent from Calgary. With my mouth gaping, I stared at the very businesslike picture of him in a suit, then back to the stoned wild-child before me.

With expected eloquence, he captured the moment: "Awesome night, dude. I've never seen a hitchhiker with a sign that said *please* before."

As Steve peeled out of the parking lot, I thought about what had just happened and said a prayer of thanks to God. Despite my poor judgment, despite the insanity of others, there I stood— shivering in an empty parking lot, but alive.

I found a pay phone outside the restaurant and dialed a friend's number collect. It was late, but I didn't care. I was out of pride, out of money, and definitely out of energy.

Thirty minutes later I sat sandwiched between two good friends in a warm truck traveling the speed limit, unraveling my epic adventure for the first of many times.

Soon I was home—dear, sweet home—and as I snuggled into my warm bed, I couldn't wipe the grin from my face. It had been a long and crazy day, but I had survived.

Tomorrow, I vowed, I would put the Green Hornet up for sale.

One glorious day Benjamin Bowler walked away from his cubicle and never looked back. He wanted to write. Now he writes stories, wears wool sweaters, and documents life to the point of neurosis. He's never been happier. When he isn't riding a snowboard, motorcycle, or airplane to obscure destinations, you'll find him hunched over a laptop, writing his first book about adventures from Mount Kilimanjaro to the back roads of the Canadian Rockies. His work has appeared in The Globe and Mail, The Calgary Herald *and numerous magazines across Canada. He lives in Calgary, Alberta, and can be reached at* **benjamin@scrollcommunications.com.**

PUBLISHER'S NOTE: While Benjamin Bowler enjoys telling this story, neither he nor the publisher condones reckless driving or the use of illegal drugs.

After the Flood

One family draws inspiration from tragedy.

By Julie Seibt

The time had come to forge a dream into reality, to travel the world for a school year with our two daughters: Taylor, eleven, and Lauren, nine. Our classroom would be the world, with a curriculum directed by Destiny, and the teacher none other than Life.

In an effort to ground our lofty ideals, my husband Ken and I joined forces with another family of four—Karen and Phil, and their children Joshua and Julia—and enrolled the children in a distance-learning program. We also enlisted the help of a teacher, Tim, who was keen to travel with us and shared our vision of education through travel. With an itinerary that attempted to balance adventure with safety and challenge with repose, we departed from our hometown of Canmore, Alberta for an adventurous year abroad.

Nothing could have prepared us for the life-altering lessons that lay ahead.

Our first destination was Europe. After a stop in England, we pushed, pulled, and dragged schoolbooks, laptops, and rock-climbing gear through Italy, where we stayed in mountain huts, stone farmhouses, and beachside villas. A few months later a locust infestation welcomed us to Egypt, along with a world peace conference in the Egyptian seaside town of Sharm el Sheik. The curriculum was packed with outdoor adventure, history, science, and politics.

Schoolbooks snapped shut for Christmas celebrations in Railay Bay, Thailand. Accessible only by boat, the isthmus of Railay is isolated from the mainland by a barrier of limestone cliffs that tower over the Andaman Sea in the province of Krabi. Spoiled from months of off-season travel, we endured our resort's compulsory elbow-to-elbow Christmas dinner and entertainment, complete with a scrawny Santa Claus and transsexual elves. A foil banner wished everybody a "Merry Christmas 2005," even though the year was actually 2004. Perhaps the sign was intended to stretch to the New Year's party, which by that time we knew to avoid.

What we didn't know was the New Year's Eve party would never happen. By then, the resorts that were packed to hundred-percent occupancy on Christmas Day would be virtually abandoned. The few people who remained would be gripped by fear and grief. For us, travelling would suddenly feel frivolous.

The catalyst would be the tsunami.

Dec. 26, 2004—Tsunami Strikes

The tsunami, born from an earthquake 1,500 kilometres from our travelling classroom, pushed through the sea like a great crocodile unleashed from its lair. It emerged on tranquil beaches with a fury that swallowed nearly two hundred and thirty thousand lives and nipped at our heels as we ran.

An excerpt from Lauren's journal records our experience:

I thought it was weird that all the time we were happily playing with our Christmas toys (three hours) the tsunami was heading straight for us. Julia's mom came running into the bungalow shouting, "Tsunami!" We thought it was a joke because we didn't even know what a tsunami was. Then she said, "Tidal wave," and we grabbed our floaties that we got from Santa.

We ran to the side of the isthmus opposite from where the biggest waves were coming. As we watched the waves come at us, they were not as big as people said they were on the other side, but we still couldn't stay there because boats might crash into us. Our two families were all together, but we didn't know where Tim (our teacher) was and we didn't know where to go. Two men gave their life jackets to me and Julia. A man that worked at the resort took us through the jungle to higher ground. It was hot and I was scared because I didn't know what could happen to us. When we got to higher ground, there were hundreds of people.

High above the vulnerable three-hundred-metre-wide strip of land where our bungalows lay, our sense of urgency gradually subsided. But fear remained. The sea in the distance was striped with angry, dark movements that we didn't understand. Thank God both families were together. But where was Tim?

The girls took turns crying, a welcome release. Eleven-year-old Joshua offered comfort: "It's okay, Taylor—even if the waves come this high, only our feet will get wet."

I watched Ken with his laptop, recalling how I had questioned his reasoning when he took the time to grab it as we fled the bungalow. Now, atop this hill of fear, he accessed international news on the Internet through GSM service on his phone.

The facts were disturbing, yet comforting compared to the rumors. CNN reported: "The largest earthquake to shake the planet in nearly forty years jolted Southeast Asia." We learned that the quake, which originated near Sumatra, Indonesia, had created a tsunami with ten-metre waves that slammed into the resort town of Phuket. We contacted our family back home by e-mail, asking them to pass along word that we were safe.

Then we saw Tim; his eyes were heavy with stories that we would hear later. At that moment he was busy directing the wounded to British doctors John and Carol Dezateux, who were administering first aid. He handed me a pen and paper to record the names of people looking for loved ones. A Thai boy was searching for his mother. A Swedish man tried to control his shaking hand as he wrote the names of his wife and two young boys on the list of missing people. Some were last seen on the beach, and had been separated as they fled the tsunami. Others had been in the ocean kayaking or diving.

An atmosphere of sharing and cooperation quickly arose. Strangers offered water to our children; a Thai family prepared pots of rice and curry to share; someone distributed canned milk and soda crackers.

We returned to our bungalows around five that afternoon to find them dry and intact. But we awoke from a fitful sleep five hours later to someone banging on the door and shouting in terror, "Big wave coming! Go to viewpoint!"

Again, we fled. For peace of mind, we resigned ourselves to spending the night on the hill under the light of a full moon. Monkeys peered down from limestone cliffs. A frog jumped on Taylor's forehead before settling under my pillow for the night; I would find it sleeping there the following morning. Soft tropical breezes caressed us with the delicate scent of frangipani blossoms, as though Nature was asking our forgiveness.

We spent the following days processing our fear, shock, and ultimately, gratitude. We walked on our favourite beaches, now littered with debris. If the peninsula of Phuket had not tempered the tsunami's rage, we would all have been dead. The "what-ifs" rocked our minds and our souls.

Several people died at Railay Bay, but thousands more perished on other Thai beaches. In all, hundreds of thousands lost their lives to the Indian Ocean tsunami.

Tim eventually shared his own story with us. He had been sipping coffee fifty metres from the beach, gazing at a perfectly calm sea under cloudless skies, when the water suddenly drained away from the shore, leaving some swimmers beached. Moments later, a seven-metre wall of water rose from the ocean and raced in, pushing boats high onto the land. As the wave drew out, Tim pulled stunned people from boats and urged them to run to high ground. The greatest danger to him was the debris that each wave hurled onto land, then dragged back out to sea.

Tim worked tirelessly for weeks after sharing this story, and then returned to Australia, where his grateful family welcomed him with open arms.

Our travelling classroom joined in a flurry of beach cleaning. A Thai man pointed to a pile of broken wood beneath three mangled long-tail boats. "That boat was our life—my family's 'rice cooker,'" he said. "It was how I made money, how I brought my children to school."

Tourists and locals united to free boats from trees, swimming pools, and restaurants. Taylor and Lauren stripped a sad-looking Christmas tree of its decorations. I shovelled sand from restaurant bathrooms and helped the reservation manager communicate with travel agents.

The beach, idyllic a few days before, was now a scene from M*A*S*H. A military helicopter carried away those in need of medical attention, while bonfires of debris spewed smoke and sparks.

The media sparked concerns about the spread of diseases like cholera and malaria. Carol Dezateux, one of the doctors Tim had referred patients to for First Aid on the day the tsunami struck, was a clinical professor of pediatric epidemiology. She offered us reassurance: unlike other areas hit by the tsunami, we had a fresh water supply, intact infrastructure, and a low-density population, all of which put us at very low risk.

With the desire to help in some way, our family decided to stay in Thailand. We dropped other travel plans, thereby putting an end to our group travel. Like schoolmates setting out on separate paths after graduation, our travelling classroom disbanded.

Some say we were brave to stay; others say we were crazy. Bravery goes to those, like Tim, who put their own lives at risk to help others. Bravery goes to those maintaining an outward calm while separated from their loved ones. Our family was very lucky to escape the fate shared by tens of thousands of others. More than anything, we felt a simple gratitude for the gift of our children and the gift of life.

Launching the Build-a-Boat Fund

We stayed in Railay Bay not only to help rebuild, but also to heal our hearts until they no longer raced at the sound of sandals running on concrete paths or at the crackle of two-way radios. We wanted to forgive the Andaman Sea for her uncharacteristic fury, to play peacefully on her newly abandoned beaches, and to witness her recovery.

Messages began to pour in from our Canadian hometown of Canmore: "Is there anything we can do to help?" This set in motion a fundraising effort built out of trust among friends. Many of our fellow Canmorites felt a connection to Railay Bay through its similarities to our own home: its natural beauty, world-class rock climbing, and its dependence on tourism. (Canmore is a mecca for outdoor adventurers, with a wilderness setting famous for climbing, kayaking, caving, and mountaineering.)

We began with a plan to replace a few long-tail boats, the traditional wooden boats Thais use for fishing and transportation. But the enthusiastic response from home inspired us to do much more.

News of the fund spread through word of mouth and the Canadian media. Children dropped their Christmas money in donation boxes; corporations and families sponsored boat-building projects; schools took on the fund as class projects. "Build-a-Boat" dinner parties were organized to raise money. A woman who had travelled in Thailand turned her photos of Railay Bay into greeting cards, then donated the proceeds from sales of the cards. The dollars rolled in, bringing with them a growing feeling of responsibility and purpose for our family journey.

We had to focus quickly to fulfill our promise to put the donations to work. The boatmen were in obvious need, but what about orphaned children and the elderly? Suddenly we found ourselves in a great sea of need with only a few life rings to toss out. To whom should they go?

We spent weeks investigating the effects of the disaster. We spoke with boatmen, who used boats for fishing, transportation, tourism, or hauling cargo, and with the presidents of their local associations. We discussed ideas with resort managers and other stakeholders in the Thai business community, and attended a meeting for non-governmental agencies at the district governor's office. Concerned that dealing with any large bureaucracy would slow us down, we avoided dealing with large non-profit groups and the government. At best, we believed, influential Thais would feel pressure to dilute the funds among too many; at worst, they might claim it was their right to retain some of the funds for their own use.

The more questions we asked, the more people knew we had some money to give. Yet they did not ask for help. It seemed that every Thai citizen we approached told us of another person's more desperate situation.

We found comfort and counsel among fellow Canadians, and among French and American people we met who had spent much of their lives in the area. Through them, we connected with well-respected Thais and formed a small group of trusted confidantes. They brought us the names of those citizens most in need. From there, we verified that those on the list did not have access to government assistance or other forms of reparation, and then we met with other fund organizers to avoid overlap. We personally met each family we gave money to. As we learned of the focus other relief efforts were taking, our own goals became clearer. We decided our mission was to build new boats for the people of Railay Bay.

The Build-a-Boat Fund Floats

Ken went to work with boatmen who had lost everything, shopping for used boats and motors. Many boats for sale were from owners who were now too afraid to return to the sea. To protect against inflated *farang* (Westerner) prices, Ken kept the company of several Thais. They began looking for boats with twenty-one-rib tails, which to us sounded more like a dish from Tony Roma's than a Thai boat designed for shallow waters and mangrove forests.

Ken's cellphone contact list started filling with names like Jewi, Jok, Leong, Sonboon, Tex, Toto, Ya, and Yoh. His backpack contained papers swollen with humidity, along with a receipt book wrinkled from use on the dusty hoods of pickup trucks, palm tree trunks, and sweaty backs. Some were papers of reciprocity, written in Thai and in English, where boatmen promised to maintain the noise-reducing and fuel-efficient features on the motors provided by Build-a-Boat. Ken ate at roadside curry stands, where he could buy lunch for nine men for the same price as one restaurant meal. He returned at the end of long days, tired but fueled by the exuberance of Thai gratitude.

Boat buying brought us to an unexpected discovery: new boats were often made from illegally harvested wood, since logging had been banned in Thailand since 1989. Thus, restoring used boats became our first priority. For new boats, we dealt only with builders who used wood bearing a government stamp of approval.

While Ken worked, I continued schooling the kids in our temporary home, the Railay Bay Resort. However, the most important lessons were those of life. One day we visited a remote village to meet the proud new owners of a boat from the Build-a-Boat fund. Our girls commented on the good fortune of the village children to have so many pets: birds in teak cages, roosters, chickens, goats, dogs, cats, and ducks running freely. We placed "I am Canadian" tattoos on the children's arms, took photos, and exchanged *wais* (a *wai* is a bow with one's hands held in a prayer position). True to their gracious culture, the eldest Thai children ensured the youngest received tattoos before anyone else.

These were indelible moments, but eleven-year-old Taylor eventually began yearning for a "normal life" again, craving friendship and English conversation with people her age. Nevertheless, she had gained something invaluable; throughout her life Taylor has carried a fear of storms and other natural phenomena, but after the tsunami she said, "Mom, I'm less afraid now." Here, she had witnessed firsthand disaster and the resiliency of life, rather than looking at it through the narrow lens of the media.

By mid February, we had accepted an invitation to Thailand's northern city of Chiang Mai, where our girls joined an international school, fulfilling Taylor's desire for change. In the affordable convenience of Chiang Mai we rented a house, cared for our family, and continued to work with the fund while personally covering all associated costs to ensure every dollar donated went directly to those in need.

Taylor and Lauren enjoyed all that came with a thriving international school, especially a "United Nations" of friends and teachers. The girls sank their teeth into academics, which included classes in Thai language and culture. Many families and staff members left for spring break and returned with stories of rebuilding villages in Krabi, providing nursing care in Indonesia, and volunteering in children's camps for orphans in Phuket. Their dedication to humankind humbled us.

From Boats to Bakeries

In Chiang Mai, serendipity brought us to Khun Gai of Bake 'n Bite Bakeries, well known locally for its irresistible cinnamon rolls, pies, and bagels. Gai had a friend in need on the island of Koh Phi Phi by the name of Bau, who had lost his resort to the tsunami, then rebuilt a simple restaurant using volunteer labour, salvaged materials, and sheer determination. Gai had decided to share her recipes and provide training to help ensure Bau's success, but neither had the money required for bakery equipment and supplies.

Meanwhile, a man named Somchai and his wife Malee, who had survived the devastation of Koh Phi Phi, were hard at work on the island of Koh Jum. Before the tsunami, limited job opportunities close to home had forced Somchai and Malee to leave their two children under the care of grandparents on Koh Jum in order to work on Phi Phi. (As we learned, it was common practice for parents working in the Thai tourism industry to be separated from their children. Sadly, the tsunami claimed many parents' lives, leaving behind at least one hundred new orphans or children who had lost their principal caregiver in the province of Krabi.)

Somchai and Malee had been lucky enough to survive the tsunami, but could not continue working on the devastated island of Koh Phi Phi. To make ends meet closer to home, they were selling grilled chicken in front of their cinderblock home in the village of Ting Rai. Gai told us about the couple's previous restaurant experience and skills, and we soon envisioned the Build-a-Boat fund branching off to help this family establish a sustainable restaurant business.

That was where Gai came in. She flew south to train Somchai, Malee, and Bau, while the Build-a-Boat fund supplied ovens, mixers, cooling racks, and baking ingredients. Within days, Bau's Garden Home Restaurant had become a favourite of foreign relief workers, who refueled with carrot muffins, cinnamon buns, and toasted sandwiches on homemade bread.

Malee and Somchai's business grew more slowly, as there were few relief workers or tourists on Koh Jum. But they never have to leave their children again.

Like a garden sprouting from a few seeds, our little fund blossomed and successfully put fifty boats in the water. The fund also replaced one house, funded the start-up of the two cafes, and replaced rusted power tools for a gifted carpenter.

Occasionally ugly weeds demanded our attention: we began to hear rumors of some men receiving two boats when before they had none. One by one, we inspected each rumor, separated idle talk from fact, and found our garden to be clean. We reminded ourselves that it is better to help than to be frozen in fear and do nothing.

The gratitude and selflessness of the Thai people prevailed. We learned of a local mechanic repairing motors at no charge after losing his own boat in the tsunami; Build-a-Boat was able to replace his boat and pay for his services on behalf of his cash-poor clients. Slowly, the wheel of economic recovery began to turn.

In June we returned to Railay Bay and savoured the sight of boats, bearing the names of donors, transporting tourists. Others hauled payloads of fish or quietly waited to bring children home from school. On a nearby island, a carpenter with gleaming power tools was rebuilding demolished bungalows, while a boat builder varnished a new boat.

By August we were ready to follow through on a promise to buy a generator for Somchai and Malee's Urban Café. But the industrious couple had another idea in mind. Malee said to us, "Business is good—we have money to buy."

One Year Later

Tragedy continued long after the waves subsided for Malee's brother Toon, a twenty-seven-year-old boatman who received a boat from the fund. We learned that his first expected child died in utero when a motorcycle taxi sidecar carrying his wife Laud tipped over on the red dirt roads of Koh Jum.

Even in his grief, Toon radiated warmth and optimism at a ceremonial launching of his boat. After a six-month tune-up and repainting, the *Urban Systems, Calgary Canada* boat was adorned with flowers as a village elder chanted prayers of safe passage.

I squeezed on board with my husband and daughters to join Toon's family in a feast of sticky rice and curried goat. The ceremony seemed to cement our role as a conduit through which Canadians and Thais worked together in a relief effort that continues to change lives—not the least our own.

When we originally left Canada, we had hoped to find an opportunity, somewhere along the way, to lend a helping hand. Little did we know how it would jump in our laps, shake our world, and allow us to embrace some of life's deepest teachings.

Ken, Julie, Taylor, and Lauren Seibt are now full-time residents of Thailand. They continue to contribute to Koh Jum through Koh Jum Beach Villas, an environmentally and socially aware housing project; learn more at **www.kohjumbeachvillas.com**.

Toon and Laud are proud parents of a healthy daughter. Malee and Somchai are successful owner/operators of the beautiful beachfront Urban Café on the property of Koh Jum Beach Villas. Through profits from his Garden Home Restaurant on Koh Phi Phi, Bau has replaced his bungalows and runs a thriving resort. Khun Gai has opened her third Bake 'n Bite location in Chiang Mai and continues in her role as mentor for Somchai and Bau.

Do you have a Great Story?

If you enjoyed this collection of stories and feel you have an outrageous, funny, heartwarming or inspirational tale that you would like to share, we would love to hear from you. Our only rules are that your story has to have some unusual, illuminating or humorous twist to it, that it's a true anecdote and that it has something to do with travel or the Great Outdoors.

We are already working on a follow-up to *A Beaver is Eating My Canoe* and we are willing to look at either story proposals or pieces that have already been written. You don't have to be a professional writer. We look forward to hearing from anybody that has a great yarn to spin.

To obtain more detailed submission guidelines, please visit Summit Studios on our web site at:

www.summitstudios.biz

Please submit stories or story proposals by e-mail, fax, or snail mail to:

SUMMIT STUDIOS
#105, 2572 Birch St.
Vancouver, BC V6H 2T4
Fax: (778) 371-8561

E-mail: submissions@summitstudios.biz

We look forward to hearing from you.

Acknowledgements

A very special thanks to my wife, Stacey, who shares my passion for travel and the outdoors. She also shares my love for great stories. Without her unconditional support and her belief in my dream to found a publishing company, it would not have been possible to share these stories with you.

A big thanks to Curtis Foreman for his help with the editing and to Kirk Seton for a fantastic book design. They are both top-notch professionals.

Thanks to Robert McCaw for the great cover image of the smirking beaver.

Thanks to my friends and family members who have offered their ideas, support, and critical feedback as this book has taken shape.

And finally, thanks to the many travellers who have contributed their stories to this book. Their willingness to share means that we're all a little richer.

Other Titles by Matt Jackson

Mugged by a Moose

Edited by Matt Jackson

Is a bad day spent outside really better than a good day at the office? This collection of twenty-three short stories aims to answer that question.

Humor/Travel • Softcover • 216 pages
$19.95 • ISBN 0973467134

"It's like Chicken Soup for the Funny Bone."

- The Kitchener-Waterloo Record

I Learned Kung Fu from a Bear Cub

Edited by Matt Jackson

Have you ever watched with disbelief as your travel plans fell apart, and been tempted to look up at the cosmos and exclaim, "Why Me?" Another volume of talcs about comic misadventures, written by twenty-five free-spirited wanderers.

Humour/Travel • Softcover • 216 pages
$19.95 • ISBN 9780973467154

About Matt Jackson

A graduate of Wilfrid Laurier's Business Administration program, Matt Jackson was lured away from the corporate world by the thrill of adventure journalism while still a university student. He is now an author, editor, photojournalist and professional speaker, and is president of Summit Studios, a publishing company specializing in books about travel and the outdoors.

Matt's first book, *The Canada Chronicles: A Four-year Hitchhiking Odyssey,* is a Canadian bestseller and won the IPPY award for best North American travel memoir in 2004. He has also been featured in more than two dozen popular magazines including *Canadian Geographic, Equinox, Explore, Photo Life* and *BBC Wildlife.*

He currently lives with his wife Stacey in Vancouver, where they spend as much time hiking and kayaking as possible.